EXCEL VBA

The Ultimate Beginner's Guide to Learn VBA Programming Step by Step

David A. Williams

© Copyright 2019 - All rights reserved.

The content contained within this book may not be reproduced, duplicated or transmitted without direct written permission from the author or the publisher.

Under no circumstances will any blame or legal responsibility be held against the publisher, or author, for any damages, reparation, or monetary loss due to the information contained within this book. Either directly or indirectly.

Legal Notice:

This book is copyright protected. This book is only for personal use. You cannot amend, distribute, sell, use, quote or paraphrase any part, or the content within this book, without the consent of the author or publisher.

Disclaimer Notice:

Please note the information contained within this document is for educational and entertainment purposes only. All effort has been executed to present accurate, up to date, and reliable, complete information. No warranties of any kind are declared or implied. Readers acknowledge that the author is not engaging in the rendering of legal, financial, medical or professional advice. The content within this book has been derived from various sources. Please consult a licensed professional before attempting any techniques outlined in this book.

By reading this document, the reader agrees that under no circumstances is the author responsible for any losses, direct or indirect, which are incurred as a result of the use of information contained within this document, including, but not limited to, — errors, omissions, or inaccuracies.

TABLE OF CONTENTS

Introduction 1

CHAPTER 1: What Can You Do With VBA? 2
    Common Uses of VBA 3

CHAPTER 2: Parts of the Program 6
    Defining the Parts of a Program 6
    Programming Blocks 6
    Using the Macro Recorder 7
    Using Subs 8
    Using Functions 9
    Comments 10

CHAPTER 3: Fundamentals Of VBA 12
    Project Explorer 12
    Properties 13
    Code 13
    Looking at the VBA Toolbox 13
    Starting the Visual Basic Editor 13
    Using Project Explorer 14

CHAPTER 4: VBA, A Primer 18
    Macro Recorder 18
    Security and Macro Storage 22

How To Enable Macros Outside A Trusted Location 25

CHAPTER 5: Working With Loops 27

The For Loop 27

For...Next Statement 31

The For Each ... Next Statement 31

Nesting Loops 33

The Exit For Statement 34

Do...Loop Statement 36

Exit Do 38

The Do While Loop 40

The Exit Do Statement 44

The Do Until Loop 46

The Exit Do Statement 48

CHAPTER 6: Working With Conditional Statements 49

If...Then...Else Statements 49

Select...Case Statement 63

Select...Case Statements Versus the If...Then...Else Statements 78

CHAPTER 7: Working With Strings 79

Points to Remember 80

Appending Strings 82

Extracting Parts of a String 83

Searching in a String 85

Removing Blanks 89

Length of a String 90

Reversing a String 91

Comparing Strings 91

Comparing Strings Using Operators 92

Comparing Strings Using Pattern Matching 94

Replacing Part of a String 97

Multiple Replaces 101

CHAPTER 8: Arrays 103

Structured Storage 103

Array Types 106

VBA Array 107

Example To Enter Student Marks 108

Example With Loops 111

Sorting An Array 112

Example For Creating A Two-Dimensional Array 113

CHAPTER 9: Error Handling And Debugging 115

The On Error Statement 116

Enabled And Active Error Handlers 118

The Resume Statement 119

Error Handling With Multiple Procedures 122

CHAPTER 10: How To Improve The Performance Of Macros 123

Close Everything Except For The VBA Essentials 123

Removing Unnecessary Selects 126

Using The With Statement To Read Object Properties 127

Using Arrays And Ranges 128

Use .Value2 Instead Of .Text or .Value 129

Avoid Using Copy And Paste 130

Use The Option Explicit Keyword To Catch
Undeclared Variables 131

CHAPTER 11: How to Redirect the Flow 132
    Using the GoTo Statement Correctly 132

CHAPTER 12: Working with Excel Workbooks and Worksheets. 134
    The Workbook Collection 134
    The Worksheet Collection 137
    Charts Collection 139

CHAPTER 13: Some Problems With Spreadsheets And How To Overcome Them 143
    Multi-User Editing 143
    Shared Workbooks 144
    Linked Workbooks 145
    Data Validation 146
    Navigation Issues 147
    Security Issues 148
    Speed Issues 148
    Enter the Database 148

CHAPTER 14: How To Use Data From Excel 152
    Property Application.ScreenUpdating 154
    Open the Source File and Read Data 154

CHAPTER 15: How to Manipulate Data In Excel 156
    How to Analyze and Manipulate Data In A Spreadsheet 158
    Different Ways To Manipulate Data 161

CHAPTER 16: Resources For VBA Help 164
    Allow Excel To Write The Code For You 164
    The Location Matters When You Ask For Help 165

Choose Online Help Over Offline Help 165

Using Code From The Internet 166

Leveraging Excel VBA User Forums 166

Leveraging on Excel VBA Blogs And Articles 167

Mining YouTube For Some Excel VBA Training Videos 169

Attending A Live Online Excel VBA Training Class 169

Dissecting Other Excel Files In Your Organization 170

Ask The Local Excel Guru 170

CHAPTER 17: Mistakes To Avoid 171

Not Using Arrays 171

Using .Select or .Activate 172

Using Variant Type 173

Not Using Application.ScreenUpdating = False 173

Referencing the Worksheet Name With a String 174

Not Qualifying the Range References 175

Writing a Big Function 177

Using Nested For or If Statements 177

Conclusion 180

References 181

Introduction

Most people use Microsoft Excel at work, and they often perform repetitive tasks. Excel VBA is an extremely helpful tool since it will help you automate mundane tasks like copying data. For this, you will need to create a function that will reduce manual work thereby increasing productivity. When you learn how to use VBA, you can learn how to manipulate and customize the data in an Excel sheet. This book covers some basic information about VBA including the different data types and variables that you can use to automate processes and functions.

This book will take you through some basic concepts of VBA and will help you master programming in Excel VBA. You will also learn how to source data in Excel from one worksheet or workbook to another without having to open the files. You can use these statements to make it easier for you to perform iterative tasks. If you want to understand how you can use VBA to improve the processes that you work on, you have come to the right place. This book will also help you learn more about how you can manipulate strings and handle any errors.

Many examples have been given across the book that will help you learn the concepts better. You should practice these examples before you write any new code. You can also use the examples in the book as a base to write larger programs.

I hope you gathered all the information you were looking for.

CHAPTER 1

What Can You Do With VBA?

VBA or Visual Basic for Applications is a combination of Microsoft Office Applications and Visual Basic which is an event-driven programming language developed by Microsoft. VBA allows you to automate numerous activities in any Microsoft application using a Macro. This helps a user save the time he or she spends to perform repetitive activities.

People use Excel VBA for multiple reasons including the following:

- Creating lists

- Creating forms and invoices

- Analyzing data

- Developing diagrams and charts using data

- Forecasting and Budgeting

There are many other tasks one can perform using Excel, but I am sure you understand what I am saying. In simple words, one can use Excel to perform different tasks since you can automate any function in Excel using VBA. For example, you may want to develop or create a program that you can use to extract or import some numbers or data, and then format that data to help you print a report. When you develop the code, you can assign the code or macro to a button or a command. This will help you complete the task in a few minutes instead of an hour.

Common Uses of VBA

There are many reasons why most companies and organizations use VBA at work. It is important to remember that it will take you some time to write the code to automate any process. Therefore, you will need to take some time out of your busy schedule and see what you can do with VBA. This section covers some of the common processes that most people use VBA for.

Automating Documents

Most people hate having to prepare a document, and it is worse when the documents that are prepared have the same content or information that must be sent to many people. In such instances, one can use the Mail Merge add-in in Excel. This add-in is used to automate a document or letter. Remember that you cannot use this option if you need to write individual emails or documents. If you need to write individual documents, you can use VBA to help you create a form that will include the necessary information. You can also include some checkboxes that a user can choose from to create or write a document.

Word processing is only one of the many tasks that you can automate using VBA. You can also write different macros or programs to help you automate some functions in a spreadsheet. For instance, you can extract data or information from the Internet onto a spreadsheet just by clicking a button. This will help you reduce the time you spend on copying the information from the Internet and pasting it in the spreadsheet in the required format.

Customizing Application Interfaces

Some features in an application do not necessarily have to make your work easier for you, and these features can be turned off. You cannot turn these features off if you need to use them occasionally for work. Therefore, instead of disabling this feature, you can write a code in VBA that will allow you to access only those features that you use for your work. For instance, you can write a program in VBA if there are some additional functions, like conditional formatting, that you will need to include in your worksheet.

You can always change the interface of an application so that it can work better for you. You can customize menu systems and toolbars, and can also change how some elements function in the interface if you want to improve the look of the application. You can also use multiple interfaces if you want to switch between different interfaces.

One of the most common uses of VBA is to improve computation speed. You can perform numerous calculations in a few seconds. You can also create equations, graphs, and functions using the data in a worksheet or workbook. There will be a need to make changes or modifications to the data in the worksheet or workbook, and we will cover these concepts a little later in the book. If there are some complicated equations in your workbook or worksheet, you can use VBA to build a code that will simplify that process. There are some iterative functions that you can use to perform these calculations.

There are cases when the numbers that you obtain through some calculations will not make too much sense. You will only be able to use the number once someone has decided what to do with it. If these decisions are repetitive, you can use VBA to write a program that will decide what to do with the number while you play Hearts on your laptop.

Adding new Application Features

Many vendors and developers never use the applications that they build. Therefore, these applications are often not up to date. You can either tweak those applications or develop new applications using VBA. You can use these new applications to complete your work in a few minutes or less. This will certainly impress your boss, and could probably lead to a promotion.

CHAPTER 2

Parts of the Program

You must follow a specific structure and syntax when you write a program in VBA. This will help the debugger understand what your code is trying to achieve. This chapter will help you understand the structural elements in a program.

Defining the Parts of a Program

A program contains every element that is required to complete a specific task. Programs can cross modules, class modules, and also create boundaries. The idea of a program came into existence when computers were first used. Programs are containers that hold specific code that is used to implement some features or perform some tasks that the user or an operating system must perform. People often have a hard time understanding what a program is since most software packages define it incorrectly. When you build or create a new project, you are not developing a new program. It is important to remember that one VBA project can include multiple programs.

Programming Blocks

Every program, including a VBA program, consists of some building blocks. Since programming is an abstract concept, most people use physical examples to explain how things work. You will need to know what the abstract elements are in a VBA program since you cannot write a program otherwise. This section will list the different elements of a VBA program.

Project

A project is used to contain the different class modules, forms and modules for a specific workbook. When it comes to Excel, a user can only view the project for the workbook that is currently open.

Module, Class Module and Forms

These elements contain the main parts of the program including procedures and class descriptions. One project can have multiple forms, modules, and class modules in it, and each of them should have a different name.

Function and Sub

The function and sub elements in a VBA program will hold all the individual lines of code. Functions will always return the value that any user requires, but a sub does not perform that action. Therefore, it is important that you allow the VBA editor to access a specific program using a Sub.

Statement

Most developers and experts call one line of code a statement.

Using the Macro Recorder

A macro recorder will allow you to record all the keystrokes and actions that you will perform when you use VBA in Excel. Remember that this will also record any incorrect keystrokes as well. This tool is often used to record any task like highlighting text or using filters.

A macro recorder can be used to perform the following tasks:

- Discover how Word performs certain tasks.
- Create a macro based on your actions.
- Help you create the basis for a more complex program.
- Decide how to break your program into tasks.

A macro recorder does not write the code for you in VBA. For example, you cannot use a macro recorder to create a program without writing some additional code. This holds for programs that require user input or for programs that are dependent on the environment and the data you use. For these tasks, you will need to add more code, but it is a good way to start developing a program. You can always get the basics of the program set by using a macro recorder.

- Start the Macro Recorder.
- Perform all the steps that you normally perform to accomplish a task.
- Stop the Macro Recorder.
- Save the macro when the Office application prompts you.
- Optionally, open the resulting macro and make any required changes.

We will look at a macro recorder in more detail later in the book.

Using Subs

You can reduce the complexity or size of the code by using a sub. This is a packaging method that is present in a Macro dialog box. You will always need to use a sub to begin the program unless the program you are writing is for a different purpose. You can also use a sub when you are writing programs that will perform specific tasks and not return any value. Subs can also be used to display some information, and it can be used to perform different tasks. It is important to remember that a sub can never return any value. You can, however, use arguments as a way to modify the information in a function by using a Sub. Alternatively, you can use global variables. A sub can be used to break a complex or large code into smaller segments or sections, which will make it easy for you and any other user to understand the code better.

Using Functions

Once you have worked extensively with the Sub procedure, you may avoid using a Function. Remember that you cannot solve every problem or automate every process using a sub. You will need to use Function for different problems when compared to a Sub. For example, you will need to use a Function if you want to return some value to the user after performing some calculations. A sub, on the other hand, is used when you want to access any external code.

A Function always returns a value, which makes it different from a Sub. It is for this reason that most programmers write functions to avoid writing repetitive code. To process a list of names, you might create a Function to process each name individually and then call that Function once for each name. The Function can provide the processed information as a return value. We will look at how we can use loops to write repetitive code.

You can also use a Function for public code that you do not want to list in the Macro dialog box. You normally do not see a Function listed in the Macro dialog box — this dialog box usually lists only Subs.

Comments

It is always a good idea to include comments in your code to help any user, including yourself, to understand the purpose behind the code.

Writing Basic Comments

Comments can be written in different ways. Some programmers write pseudo-comments against blocks of code since this is one of the easiest ways to use a comment. Developers always add comments to any program that they are writing since it will provide a user with an understanding of why a specific line of code was written. These comments also provide some information on the updates made to the program. This is when a developer begins to write better programs.

The most important comment that you should include in your code is why you are writing the program. It is important to explain to other users why your program was written in a specific way. You should never leave vague comments since that will not help a user understand why you chose the method you did to write the code. These comments will also help you when you decide to update the code you have written. Using the comments, you can also understand why you must update the code.

A good programmer should always include the mistakes that they made while writing the code. This will help another programmer understand what they should avoid doing to improve their code. These comments will also help you when you choose to update the program that you have written.

Knowing when to use Comments

It is always a good idea to use comments wherever you think you should include them. It is a difficult task to include a comment and type it out in the code window, but it is always good to do so to explain what the purpose of the program is. It will take you some time to write a good comment, and it may also be difficult since you may wonder why you wrote the program in a specific way. If you do not have a good number of comments in your program, you may be unable to update it since you have no idea what the purpose of a function is. There will come a time when you will need to write the code from scratch because you have no idea what you were trying to do.

Writing Good Comments

A comment is said to be good if any user can understand what it means. You should always avoid using jargon, and explain the function of the statement in simple terms. If you want to explain every line of code, you can do this since it will help another user understand why you chose to act in a specific way.

CHAPTER 3

Fundamentals Of VBA

VBA is a visual programming environment. That is, you see how your program will look before you run it. Its editor is very visual, using various windows to make your programming experience easy and manageable. You will notice slight differences in the appearance of the editor when you use it with Vista as compared to older or newer versions of Windows. Regardless of which version of Windows you use or which Office Product you use, the Visual Basic Editor has the same appearance, same functionality, and same items.

The IDE is like a word processor, database form or a spreadsheet. The IDE, like every other application editor, has special features that make it easy to work with data. Apart from that, the IDE can also be used to write special instructions that help with data manipulation and analysis. VBA will follow the instructions in the program. The IDE in VBA consists of a toolbar, menu system, a Properties window, a Project Explorer window and a Code window. Below is a summary of what each Window contains.

Project Explorer

This window provides a list of the items or objects that are in your project. These items contain the document elements that are present in a single file. This application exists within a file, which you will see in the Project Explorer window.

Properties

When you select an object, the Properties window will give you all the information you need about that object. For instance, this window will tell you whether the object is empty or whether there are some words in it.

Code

Eventually, you will need to write some code, which will make the application work. This window will contain the special words that will tell the editor what it needs to do. This space is analogous to a to-do list or an algorithm.

Looking at the VBA Toolbox

You will not have to write a program for every task that you want Excel to perform. The IDE also allows you to use forms, which are similar to the forms that you use to perform different tasks. In the case of VBA, you will decide what should appear on the form and also decide how the form should act when a user enters some data into the form. VBA allows you to use the toolbox to create a form. This toolbox contains controls used to create forms.

Each Toolbox button performs a unique task. For example, when you click one button, a text box may appear on the screen. If you click another button, a mathematical operation may take place.

Starting the Visual Basic Editor

One can start the Visual Basic Editor in different ways depending on the application you are using. The newer versions of the Office

Product use a different approach when compared to the older versions.

- Step 1: Go to Option "View" on the toolbar.
- Step 2: In the drop-down list, select "Record Macro."
- Step 3: The interface will open, and you can begin typing the code for the worksheet you are in.

Using Project Explorer

The Project Explorer will appear in the Project Explorer Window, and you can use this to interact with different objects that make up the project. Every project is an individual file that you can use to hold your program or at least some pieces of it. This project will reside in the Office document, which you are using. Therefore, when you open the document, you also open the project. We will look at how programs and projects interact with each other in later chapters. The Project Explorer works like the left pane in Windows Explorer.

The Project Explorer lists the different objects you are using in the project. These objects depend on the type of application you are working with. For example, if you are working with Word, you see documents and document templates. Likewise, if you are working with Excel, you will come across different workbooks and worksheets. Regardless of the type of application you work with, the Project Explorer will be used in the same way.

A project can contain modules, class modules and forms. Let us look at the description of these objects:

- Forms These contain some user interface elements that allow you to interact with a user and collect the necessary information.

- Modules - These contain the nonvisual parts of your code or application. For instance, you can use a module to store some calculations.

- Class modules - These contain objects that you want to develop, and you can use a class module to create new data types.

Working with Special Entries

You can sometimes see some special entries in the Project Explorer. For instance, when you work on a Word document, you will see a References folder that will contain the references that the Word document makes. This contains a list of templates that the document uses to format the data in the document.

In many cases, you cannot modify or manipulate the objects in the folders. This is the case when Word document objects use a Reference folder. This folder is only available to provide information. If you want to modify or develop a referenced template, you should look for the object in the Project Explorer window. We will not discuss these concepts in the book since you do not work with these often.

Using the Properties Window

Most objects that you select in the IDE in VBA always have properties that describe the objects in a specific way. The "Property values are up" section talks about the properties that you have not worked with before. The following section will provide more information about the Properties Window.

Understanding Property Types

A property will always describe the object. When you look at an object, you will assume something about the product depending on whether the object is red, yellow, or green. In the same way, every

VBA object has a specific type. One of the most common types is text. The property of every form is text, and this text appears at the top or bottom of the form when a user opens it. Another common property type is a Boolean value.

Getting Help with Properties

Do not expect to memorize every property for every object that VBA applications can create. Experts themselves cannot remember the properties for objects in different VBA applications. If you want to learn more about a specific object or property, select the property and press F1. VBA will display a Help window that will describe the functions or the properties of the object.

Using the Code Window

The Code Window is the space where you will write the code for your application. This window works like every other text editor that you have used, except that you type according to the syntax. When you open the Code window, you will not be able to view the Project Explorer and Property windows. You can display the Project Explorer window and Property by following the path: View -> Project Explorer and View ->Properties Window commands.

Opening an Existing Code Window

Sometimes you will not have the time to complete the code for an application and will need to work on it later. You must look for the module you want to use in the Project Explorer, and click on that. This will open an existing code window. Double-click the name of the module that you want to enter. You will see the code in the IDE window. This Code window will also appear when you want to perform a variety of tasks.

Creating a New Code Window

When you want to develop a new module in an existing document or template, you should open a new code window by using the following path: Insert -> Module or Insert -> Class Module command. Once you save this class module or module, it will always be in the Project Explorer with every other module that is in your project.

It is easier to execute one line of code at a time to understand where you may have made an error. You can do this by using the Immediate Window. You will always find this window at the bottom of the IDE, and it will not contain any information until you type something in it.

A developer spends a lot of time using the immediate window to check if there are any errors in the applications they are developing. You can use the immediate window to check with VBA if the function you have written produces the required value. To try this feature, type String1 = "Hello World" in the Immediate window and then press Enter. Now type '? String1' and then press Enter. Here, you have asked the editor to create a variable called String1 and assign it a value of Hello World. You can use the '?' operator to check the value assigned to the variable String1.

CHAPTER 4

VBA, A Primer

Microsoft Office products like PowerPoint, Word, Outlook, FrontPage, Visio, Access, Project, Excel and some other third-party programs support VBA. If you have Microsoft Office on your device, you have VBA. VBA works similarly on all Microsoft products except for Access. The differences only relate to the specific objects of every application. For example, if you are using a spreadsheet object, you can only use it in Excel. VBA is currently based on VB 6.0, but there is a possibility that the future releases will migrate towards .net.

The focus of this book is how you can use VBA in Excel. VBA enhances the use of Excel by providing valuable features that you will not find with Excel formulas.

Macro Recorder

You can write macros in VBA in the same way that you would write code in VB. The concepts of structures, variables, expressions, subprocedures, etc. are the same for both VB and VBA. The problem with VBA is that you will need to refer to every object you are writing code for. For example, if you were writing code for a specific cell in a worksheet, you will need to refer to that specific cell in your code. You are often unaware of what the names of these objects are and the attributes that you can control. The Macro Recorder solves this problem.

The macro recorder helps you develop a new macro in Excel quickly and easily. You must start the recorder and perform the necessary actions. The macro recorder will write the code for you. Alternatively, you can also run the VBA editor, which will allow you to insert a new module. This will give you a blank sheet on which you can write your macro. If you have already written the macro, you do not have to insert a new module. You will only need to add code to an existing module.

You will need to make some changes to the code written by the macro recorder. This is important to do when you need to change the cell references from absolute to relative or when you need the user form to interact with the user. If you have read the earlier version of the book, you will be familiar with VBA in Excel and some of the syntaxes and structures. Additionally, you must understand the differences between relative and absolute addressing.

VBA is different from VB in the sense that it is not a standalone language. VBA can only run through another product. For example, every VBA application you write in Excel can only run within Excel. This means that you will need to run Excel, then load the macro after which the compiler will execute the macro. The VBA applications are all stored in the spreadsheet that they were written in. You can also store VBA application in a way that will allow you to refer to them in other worksheets or workbooks.

When the application is loaded into Excel, you can invoke the application in many ways. Let us look at a few ways to run the macro:

1. You can assign a key to the macro when you record the macro. You can then invoke the macro by pressing Ctrl-"key." If the key is "a," your shortcut will be Ctrl+a. You

must remember that the macro shortcut will override the default meaning of the Ctrl+a shortcut. You should also note that Ctrl/a and Ctrl/A are different.

2. You can either include an object or a button on the spreadsheet to call the macro. Go to the Forms window using the path Menu->View->Toolbars->Forms and select the command button. Now, draw the button on the spreadsheet. Choose the macro that you want to link to the button when the dialog box or prompt opens. You can also include pictures and other objects and assign macros to them.

3. Select the macro from the menu and run it. Go to the Macros section using the following path Menu->Tools->Macro->Macros and choose the macro you want to run.

4. You can also use the VBA editor to run the macro. You can either click on the run button to run the macro or go through each line of the code while giving yourself time to debug the code. When you are debugging the code, you should move the VBA editor into a pane adjacent to the spreadsheet and execute the code to see what is happening.

If you choose to name a macro "Sub Auto_Open()," this macro will run when you load or open the spreadsheet. This will only happen if you have enabled macros.

As mentioned in the previous chapter, the macro recorder is an important and useful tool in Excel. This tool will record every action that you perform in Excel. You only need to record a task once using the macro recorder, and you can execute that same task a million times by clicking a button. If you do not know how to program a specific task in Excel, you can use the Macro Recorder to help you understand what you need to do. You can then open the Visual Basic Editor once you have recorded the task to see how you can program it.

You cannot perform many tasks when you use the Macro Recorder. For instance, you cannot use the macro recorder to loop through data. The macro recorder also uses more code than you need, which will slow the process down.

Record A Macro

- Go to the Menu Bar and move the Developer Tab, and click the button to Record the Macro.

- Enter the name of the macro.

- Choose the workbook where you want to use the macro. This means that the macro can only be used in the current workbook.

- If you store the macro in a personal macro workbook, you can access the macro in all your workbooks. This is only because Excel stores the macro in a hidden workbook, which will open automatically when it starts. If you store the macro in a new workbook, you can use the macro only in the opened workbook.

- Click OK.

- Now, right click on the active cell in the worksheet. Ensure that you do not select any other cell. Click format cells.

- Select the percentage.

- Click OK.

- Now, select the stop recording.

You have successfully recorded your macro using the macro recorder.

Run The Recorded Macro

You will now need to test the macro and see if you can change the format of the numbers to percentage.

- Enter any numbers between 0 and 1 in the spreadsheet.
- Select the numbers.
- Move to the Developer tab, and click Macros.
- Now click run.

See The Macro

If you want to look at the macro, you should open the Visual Basic Editor.

The macro, called Module 1, is placed in a module. The code that is placed in the module is always available to the full workbook. This means you can change the format for the numbers in all the sheets in the workbook. If you assign a macro to the command button, you should remember that the macro would only be available for that specific sheet.

Security and Macro Storage

For every Microsoft Office application, there are three security levels for macros. The macro security level is always set to high by default. To change the security of your macro, go to the security tab and make your selection. Go to Menu->Tools->Security Tab->Macro Security.

The three security levels for macros are:

1. High: The macros that are signed by a trusted source will run in Excel. If there is any unsigned macro, it will automatically be disabled.

2. Medium: This is the recommended setting since you can choose to enable or disable a macro.

3. Low: This is not recommended since the macros are loaded into the workbook without notifying the user.

If you know you will be using macros, you should set the security of the macros to medium. When you load the spreadsheet, Excel will ask you if you want to enable or disable a macro. If you know that a specific sheet contains a macro and you know who wrote it, you can enable it.

Since some macros are set to run when you open a spreadsheet, it is not possible for you to always have the chance to examine the macro before you enable it. It is important to remember that an Excel Macro virus is very rare. This is because a macro is only available on the spreadsheet where it was written. Macros are always stored in the workbook by default and every time you load the workbook, and the macros are loaded.

When you create a macro for the first time, you can decide where to store the macro. The best choices are:

1. This Workbook: The macro is stored in the worksheet where it is written. Anybody who has access to the worksheet can access the macro.

2. Personal Macro Workbook: All the macros on your PC are stored in this workbook. Only when you copy the macro and save it with the spreadsheet will others be able to view the macro.

You can use the VBA editor to see where the macros are stored. The Project Explorer Window, on the upper left of the screen, shows you where the files are placed and their hierarchy. You can use the Explorer to view, move, copy or delete a macro.

How To Add A Trusted Location

As mentioned earlier, you can save the workbooks with macros in a folder that you mark as a trusted location. If you save a workbook in that folder, the macros will always be enabled. The developers suggest that you should always have a trusted location in your hard drive. Remember that you can never trust the location on a network drive.

If you want to specify a trusted location, you should follow the steps given below:

1. Go to the Developer Tab and click on Macro Security.

2. Move to the left navigation pane in the Trust Center and choose the Trusted Location.

3. If you want to save the file on a network drive, you should add that location into the trusted locations.

4. Go to 'My Networks' in the Trusted Location dialog box and click the 'Add New Location' button.

5. You will see the list of Trusted Locations in a dialog box.

6. Now click the Browse button and go to the parent folder of the folder that you want to make a trusted location. Now click on the Trusted Folder. You will not find the name of the Folder in the text box, but click OK. The correct name will come in the Browse dialog box.

7. If you want to include the subfolders in the selected folder, you should select the radio button against the 'Subfolders of this location are also trusted' option.

8. Now, click OK to add the folder to the list.

How To Enable Macros Outside A Trusted Location

When you do not save an Excel workbook in a trusted location, excel will always rely on the macro settings. In Excel 2003, a macro could have a low, medium, high or very high security. These settings were later renamed by the developers in Microsoft. If you want to access the macro settings, you should go to the Developers Tab and choose Macro Security. Excel will then display the Macro Settings dialog box. You should select the 'Disable All Macros with Notification' option. Let us look at the description of the options in the dialog box.

Disable All Macros Without Notification

This setting will not allow any macro to run. If you do not always want to run the macro when you open the workbook, you should choose this setting. However, since you are still learning how to use macros and work with them, you should not use this setting. This setting is equivalent to the Very High Security that is found in Excel 2003. If you choose this setting, you can only run macros if they are saved in a Trusted Location.

Disable All Macros With Notification

This setting is like the Medium security setting in Excel 2003. This is the recommended setting that you should use. If you use this setting, Excel will ask you if you want to enable to disable a macro when you open a workbook. You may often choose this option if you are a beginner. In Excel 2010, you will see a message in the message area, which states that the macros have been disabled. You can either choose to enable or disable the content in the workbook by choosing that option.

Disable All Macros Except Digitally Signed Macros

If you wish to use this setting, you should always use a digital signing tool like VeriSign or any other provider to sign your macro. If you are going to sell your macros to other parties, you should use this security option. This is a hassle if you want to write macros only for your use.

Enable All Macros

Experts suggest that you do not use this option since dangerous codes can also run on your system. This setting is equivalent to the Low-security option in Excel 2003 and is the easiest option to use. This option will open your system up to attacks from malicious viruses.

Disabling All Macros With Notification

Experts suggest that you set your macro to disable all content after it gives you a notification. If you save a workbook with a macro using this setting, you will see a security warning right above the formula bar when you open the workbook. If you know that there are macros in the workbook, all you need to do is click 'Enable Content.' You can click on the X on the far right of the bar if you do not want to enable any of the macros in the workbook.

If you do forget to enable the macro and then attempt to run that macro, Excel will indicate that the macro will not run since you have disabled all macros in the workbook. If this happens, you should reopen the workbook to enable the macros again.

CHAPTER 5

Working With Loops

One of the most powerful and basic programming tools available in VBA is a loop. This tool is used across many programming languages where the programmer wants to repeat a block of code until a condition holds true or until a specific point. If the condition is false, the loop will break and the section of code after the loop is executed. By using loops, you can write a few lines of code and achieve significant output.

The For Loop

For Loop

Most people use the For Loop in VBA. There are two forms of the For Loop – For Next and For Each In Next. The For Loop will move through a series of data in a sequence. You can use the Exit statement to end the For Loop at any point. The loop will continue to run until the condition is met. When the final condition is met, the editor will move to the next statement in the program, which is the natural direction.

Let us look at the syntax of the loop:

The For ... Next loop has the following syntax:

For counter = start_counter To end_counter

'Do something here (your code)

Next counter

In the syntax above, we are initializing the counter variable, which will maintain the loop. This counter variable will be set to a value that is equal to the start_counter that will be the beginning of the loop. This variable will increase in number until it meets the end condition which is the end_counter variable. The loop will continue to run until the value of the counter is equal to the value of the end_counter variable. This loop will execute once until the values match, after which the loop will stop.

The explanation above can be slightly confusing, therefore let us look at a few examples that you can use to understand the For Loop better. Before we look at the examples, follow the steps given below:

    Open a new workbook and save it using the .xlsm extension.

    Now, press Alt+F11 to launch the Visual Basic Editor screen.

    Now, insert a new module.

Example 1

[1]In this example, we will display a number using a message box.

Sub Loop1()

Dim StartNumber As Integer

Dim EndNumber As Integer

---

[1] 7 Examples of For Loops in Microsoft Excel VBA | VBA. (2019). Retrieved from https://www.exceltip.com/vba/for-loops-with-7-examples.html

EndNumber = 5

    For StartNumber = 1 To EndNumber

    MsgBox StartNumber & " is " & "Your StartNumber"

    Next StartNumber

End Sub

In the above code, the StartNumber and EndNumber variables are declared as integers, and the StartNumber is the start of your loop. The values that you enter in the loop can be anywhere in between the StartNumber and EndNumber. The code will start from StartNumber, which is 1, and end at EndNumber which is 5. Once the code runs, the following message will be displayed on the screen.

Example 2

[2]In this example, we will fill values in the Active worksheet.

Sub Loop2()

'Fills cells A1:A56 with values of X by looping' --- Comment

'Increase the value of X by 1 in each loop' --- Comment

---

[2] 7 Examples of For Loops in Microsoft Excel VBA | VBA. (2019). Retrieved from https://www.exceltip.com/vba/for-loops-with-7-examples.html

Dim X As Integer

For X = 1 To 56

Range("A" & X).Value = X

Next X

End Sub

You will see the following output.

For...Next Statement

The For...Next Loop[3] will repeat a statement or a block of code for a specific number of iterations. The syntax for the loop is as follows:

For counter_variable = start_value To end_value

[block of code]

Next counter_variable

Let us look at a simple example of how to use this loop.

Sub forNext1()

Dim i As Integer

Dim iTotal As Integer

iTotal = 0

For i = 1 To 5

iTotal = i + iTotal

Next i

MsgBox iTotal

End Sub

The For Each ... Next Statement

If you want to repeat a block of code for every object or variable in a group, you should use the For Each...Next Loop. This statement will

---

[3] 7 Examples of For Loops in Microsoft Excel VBA | VBA. (2019). Retrieved from https://www.exceltip.com/vba/for-loops-with-7-examples.html

repeat the execution of a block of code or statements for every element in the collection. The loop will stop when every element in the collection is covered. The execution will immediately move to that section of code that is immediately after the Next statement. The syntax of the loop is as follows:

For Each object_variable In group_object_variable

[block of code]

Next object_variable

Example 1

[4]In the example below, the loop will go through every worksheet in the workbook. VBA will execute the code which will protect the worksheets with a password. In this example, the variable ws is the Worksheet Object variable. The group or collection of worksheets is present in this workbook.

Sub forEach1()

Dim ws As Worksheet

For Each ws In ThisWorkbook.Worksheets

ws.Protect Password:="123"

Next ws

End Sub

---

[4] 7 Examples of For Loops in Microsoft Excel VBA | VBA. (2019). Retrieved from https://www.exceltip.com/vba/for-loops-with-7-examples.html

Example 2

[5]In the example below, the VBA will iterate through every cell in the range A1:A10. The code will set the background color of every cell to yellow. In this example, rCell is the Range Object variable, and the collection or group of cells is present in Range("A1:A10").

Sub forEach2()

Dim rCell As Range

For Each rCell In ActiveSheet.Range("A1:A10")

rCell.Interior.Color = RGB(255, 255, 0)

Next rCell

End Sub

Nesting Loops

If you want to include more than one condition in a loop, you can use nesting. You can create a nested loop by adding one loop to another. You can add an infinite number of loops if you are creating a nested loop. You can also nest one type of a loop inside another type of loop.

If you are using a For Loop, it is important that the inner loop is completed first. It is only after the inner loop is fully complete that the statements below the Next statement of the inner loop are executed. Alternatively, you can nest one type of control structure in another.

---

[5] 7 Examples of For Loops in Microsoft Excel VBA | VBA. (2019). Retrieved from https://www.exceltip.com/vba/for-loops-with-7-examples.html

In the example below, we will use an IF statement in a WITH statement that is within a For...Each Loop. VBA will go through every cell in the range A1:A10. If the value of the cell exceeds 5, VBA will color the cell as Yellow. Otherwise, it will color the cells red.

Sub nestingLoops()

Dim rCell As Range

For Each rCell In ActiveSheet.Range("A1:A10")

With rCell

If rCell > 5 Then

.Interior.Color = RGB(255, 255, 0)

Else

.Interior.Color = RGB(255, 0, 0)

End If

End With

Next rCell

End Sub

The Exit For Statement

The Exit For statement can be used to exit the For Loop without completing the full cycle. This means that you will be exiting the For Loop early. This statement will instruct VBA to stop the execution of the loop and move to the section or block of code at the end of the loop, or the code that follows the Next statement. In the case that you are using a Nested Loop, the VBA compiler will stop executing the code in the inner loop, and begin to execute the statements in the outer loop. You should use this statement when you want to terminate the loop once it has satisfied a condition or reached a specific value. This statement can also be used to break an endless loop after a certain point.

Let us look at the following example:

In the example below, if the value of Range("A1") is blank, the value of the variable iTotal will be 55. If Range("A1") has the value 5, VBA will terminate the loop when the counter reaches the value 5. At this point, the value of iTotal will be 15. You should note that the loop will run until the counter value reaches 5, after which it will exit the loop.

Sub exitFor1()

Dim i As Integer

Dim iTotal As Integer

iTotal = 0

For i = 1 To 10

iTotal = i + iTotal

If i = ActiveSheet.Range("A1") Then

Exit For

End If

Next i

MsgBox iTotal

End Sub

Do...Loop Statement

We have at what the Do...Loop statement is and how you can use it in Excel VBA. We will now look at the syntax and understand every part of the syntax. There are some examples and exercises in this section that will help you master the Do...Loop statement.

Syntax

Type 1

Do { While | Until } condition

    [statements]

    [Continue Do]

    [statements]

    [Exit Do]

    [statements]

Loop

Type 2

Do

    [statements]

    [Continue Do]

    [statements]

    [Exit Do]

    [statements]

Loop { While | Until } condition

Understanding The Parts

Term	Definition
Do	This term is necessary to include since this starts the Do Loop.
While	This is required unless you use UNTIL in the loop. This keyword will ensure that the editor runs the loop until the condition is false.
Until	This keyword is necessary unless you are using the WHILE keyword. This will ensure that the editor will run the loop until the condition holds true.
Condition	This is optional, but it should always be a Boolean expression. If the condition is nothing, the editor will treat it as false.
Statements	These are optional. You can add one or more statements that you want the editor to repeat until the condition holds true.
Continue Do	This is also an optional statement. If you use this statement in the loop, the editor will move to the next iteration of the loop.
Exit Do	This is optional, and if you use it, the editor will move out of the Do Loop.
Loop	This keyword is necessary since it terminates the loop.

You should use the Do...Loop structure if you want to repeat a set of statements infinitely until the condition holds true. If you want to repeat the statements in the loop for a specific number of times, you should use the For...Next statements. You can either use the Until or While keywords when you specify a condition, but you should never use both.

You can place the condition either at the start or at the end of the loop. The first book mentions which structure you should use depending on when you want to test the condition. If you want to test the condition at the beginning, the loop does not have to run even once. If you test the condition at the end of the loop, the statements in the body of the loop will run at least once. This condition is a Boolean value and is often a comparison of two values. These values can be of any data type that the editor can convert to Boolean.

You can nest a Do loop by adding another loop in it. You can also nest different control structures within the Do Loop. These concepts have been covered in the first book of the series.

You should remember that the Do...Loop structure is more flexible than the While...End While statement. This is because the former allows you to decide if you want to end the loop when the condition first becomes true or when it stops being true. You also can test the condition either at the start or the end of the loop.

Exit Do

You can use the Exit Do statement as an alternative way to exit the Do...Loop. The VBA Compiler will now execute the statements that are written immediately after the loop. The Exit Do is used if you nest conditional statements within the loop. If you know that there is some condition that is unnecessary or makes it impossible for the editor to evaluate the statements within the loop. You can use this statement if you want to check for a condition that can lead to an endless loop. This statement will help you exit the loop immediately. You can use any number of Exit Do statements in the Do...Loop structure.

When you use the Exit Do statement in a nest Do loop, the editor will move from the statements within the innermost loop to the next level of nesting statements.

Example 1

[6]In the example below, the editor will run the statements in the loop only when the index variable is greater than 10. The Until keyword will end the loop.

Dim index As Integer = 0

Do

    Debug.Write(index.ToString & " ")

    index += 1

Loop Until index > 10

Debug.WriteLine("")

The output will be,

0 1 2 3 4 5 6 7 8 9 10

Example 2

[7]In the example below, we will use a While clause instead of the Until clause. The editor will test the condition at the start of the loop.

---

[6] Do...Loop Statement (Visual Basic). (2019). Retrieved from https://docs.microsoft.com/en-us/dotnet/visual-basic/language-reference/statements/do-loop-statement

```
Dim index As Integer = 0
Do While index <= 10
    Debug.Write(index.ToString & " ")
    index += 1
Loop
Debug.WriteLine("")
```

The output will be,

0 1 2 3 4 5 6 7 8 9 10

The Do While Loop

You can use the Do While Loop to repeat a block of code or statements indefinitely as long as the value of the condition holds true. VBA will stop executing the block of code when the condition returns the value False. The condition can either be tested at the start or at the end of the loop. The Do While...Loop statement is where the condition is tested at the start while the Do...Loop While the statement is the condition that is tested at the end of the loop. When the condition at the start of the loop is not met, the former loop will not execute the block of code in the loop. The latter statement will function at least once since the condition is at the end of the loop.

---

[7] Do...Loop Statement (Visual Basic). (2019). Retrieved from https://docs.microsoft.com/en-us/dotnet/visual-basic/language-reference/statements/do-loop-statement

Do While…Loop Statement

The syntax for the loop is:

Do While [Condition]

[block of code]

Loop

Do…Loop While Statement

The syntax for the loop is:

Do

[block of code]

Loop While [Condition]

The loops are explained below with the help of examples.

Example 1

[8]In the example below, the condition is tested at the beginning of the loop. Since the condition is not met, the loop will not execute, and the value of iTotal will be zero.

Sub doWhile1()

Dim i As Integer

Dim iTotal As Integer

i = 5

---

[8] Do...Loop Statement (Visual Basic). (2019). Retrieved from https://docs.microsoft.com/en-us/dotnet/visual-basic/language-reference/statements/do-loop-statement

iTotal = 0

Do While i > 5

iTotal = i + iTotal

i = i - 1

Loop

MsgBox iTotal

End Sub

Example 2

[9]In the example below, the condition is only tested at the end of the function. Since the condition is true, the loop will execute once. It will terminate after that since the value of I will reduce to 4, and the variable iTotal will return the value 5.

Sub doWhile2()

Dim i As Integer

Dim iTotal As Integer

i = 5

iTotal = 0

Do

iTotal = i + iTotal

---

[9] Do...Loop Statement (Visual Basic). (2019). Retrieved from https://docs.microsoft.com/en-us/dotnet/visual-basic/language-reference/statements/do-loop-statement

i = i - 1

Loop While i > 5

MsgBox iTotal

End Sub

Example 3

[10]In this example, we will replace the blanks in a range of cells with underscores.

Sub doWhile3()

Dim rCell As Range

Dim strText As String

Dim n As Integer

'rCell is a Cell in the specified Range which contains the strText

'strText is the text in a Cell in which blank spaces are to be replaced with underscores

'n is the position of blank space(s) occurring in a strText

For Each rCell In ActiveSheet.Range("A1:A5")

strText = rCell

---

[10] Do...Loop Statement (Visual Basic). (2019). Retrieved from https://docs.microsoft.com/en-us/dotnet/visual-basic/language-reference/statements/do-loop-statement

'the VBA InStr function returns the position of the first occurrence of a string within another string. Using this to determine the position of the first blank space in the strText.

n = InStr(strText, " ")

Do While n > 0

'blank space is replaced with the underscore character in the strText

strText = Left(strText, n - 1) & "_" & Right(strText, Len(strText) - n)

'Use this line of code instead of the preceding line, to remove all blank spaces in the strText

'strText= Left(strText, n - 1) & Right(strText, Len(strText) - n)

n = InStr(strText, " ")

Loop

rCell = strText

Next

End Sub

The Exit Do Statement

The Exit Do Statement can be used to exit the Do While Loop before you complete the cycle. The Exit Do statement will instruct VBA to stop executing the lines of code in the loop and move to the block of code that is immediately after the loop. If it is a nested loop, the statement will instruct VBA to execute the lines of code in the outer loop. You can use an infinite number of Exit Do statements in a loop, and this statement is useful when you want to terminate the loop once you obtain the desired value. This is similar to the Exit For statement.

Let us look at the following example[11]. In this example, the block of code will not be executed if the cell A1 contains a number between 0 and 11 since the condition states that the loop should be terminated if the value of 'i' is equal to the value in Cell A1.

Sub exitDo1()

Dim i As Integer

Dim iTotal As Integer

iTotal = 0

Do While i < 11

iTotal = i + iTotal

i = i + 1

If i = ActiveSheet.Range("A1") Then

Exit Do

End If

Loop

MsgBox iTotal

End Sub

---

[11] Do...Loop Statement (Visual Basic). (2019). Retrieved from https://docs.microsoft.com/en-us/dotnet/visual-basic/language-reference/statements/do-loop-statement

The Do Until Loop

The block of code in the Do Until loop is executed repeatedly until a specific condition is true. You can test the condition in the system either at the start or at the end of the loop. The Do Until Loop statement will test the condition at the start of the loop while the Do Loop Until Statement will test the condition at the end of the loop. In the former statement, the block of code within the loop is not executed even once if the condition is false. This means that the condition must hold true from the start. In the latter statement, the block of code within the loop will execute at least once even if the condition is false since the condition is at the end of the loop.

Do Until...Loop Statement

The syntax for the statement is below:

Do Until [Condition]

[block of code]

Loop

Do...Loop Until Statement

The syntax for the statement is below:

Do

[block of code]

Loop Until [Condition]

Let us understand these statements better using the following examples:

Example 1

[12]In this example, we are instructing VBA to color a blank cell until the compiler reaches a non-empty cell. If the first cell is a non-empty cell, the code in the body of the loop will not be executed since the condition is mentioned at the start of the loop.

Sub doUntil1()

Dim rowNo As Integer

rowNo = 1

Do Until Not IsEmpty(Cells(rowNo, 1))

Cells(rowNo, 1).Interior.Color = RGB(255, 255, 0)

rowNo = rowNo + 1

Loop

End Sub

---

[12] Do...Loop Statement (Visual Basic). (2019). Retrieved from https://docs.microsoft.com/en-us/dotnet/visual-basic/language-reference/statements/do-loop-statement

Example 2

[13]In this example, we are instructing VBA to color a blank cell until the compiler reaches a non-empty cell. If the first cell is a non-empty cell, the code in the body of the loop will only be executed once because the condition is only mentioned at the end of the loop.

Sub doUntil2()

Dim rowNo As Integer

rowNo = 1

Do

Cells(rowNo, 1).Interior.Color = RGB(255, 255, 0)

rowNo = rowNo + 1

Loop Until Not IsEmpty(Cells(rowNo, 1))

End Sub

The Exit Do Statement

You can exit the Do Until loop without executing all the commands in the body of the loop using the Exit Do statement. This function is similar to what was done in the Do While Loop.

---

[13] Do...Loop Statement (Visual Basic). (2019). Retrieved from https://docs.microsoft.com/en-us/dotnet/visual-basic/language-reference/statements/do-loop-statement

CHAPTER 6

Working With Conditional Statements

There are two conditional statements that you can use in VBA:

1. If...Then...Else

2. Select...Case

In both these conditional statements, VBA will need to evaluate one or more conditions after which the block of code between the parentheses is executed. These statements are executed depending on what the result of the evaluation is.

If...Then...Else Statements

This conditional statement will execute a block of statements or code when the condition is met.

Multiple-line Statements

If condition Then

statements

ElseIf elseif_condition_1 Then

elseif_statements_1

ElseIf elseif_condition_n Then

elseif_statements_n

Else

else_statements

End If

Let us break the statements down to understand what each part of the block of code written above means.

If Statement

If you want to write a multiple-line syntax, like the example above, the first line of the code should only contain the 'If' statement. We will cover the single-line syntax in the following section.

Condition

This is an expression that could either be a string or numeric. The compiler will evaluate this condition and return either true or false. It is necessary to define a condition.

Statements

These statements make up the block of code that the compiler will execute if the condition is true. If you do not specify a statement, then the compiler will not execute any code even if the condition is true.

ElseIf

This is a clause that can be used if you want to include multiple conditions. If you have an ElseIf in the code, you need to specify the elseif_condition. You can include an infinite number of ElseIf and elseif_conditions in your code.

elseif_condition

This is an expression that the compiler will need to evaluate. The result of the expression should either be true or false.

Elseif_statements

These statements or blocks of code are evaluated if the compiler returns the result true for the elseif_condition. If you do not specify a statement, then the compiler will not execute any code even if the condition is true.

The Else -> condition and elseif_conditions are always tested in the order they are written in. The code that is written immediately after a condition is executed if the condition holds true. If no conditions in the elseif_conditions returns the value the true, the block of code after the **Else** clause will be executed. You can choose to include the Else in the If...Then...Else statement.

else_statements

These statements are the blocks of code written immediately after the Else statement.

End If

This statement terminates the execution of the statements in the If...Then...Else block of code. It is essential that you use these keywords only at the end of the block of code.

Nesting

You can nest the If...Then...Else statements in a loop using the Select...Case or VBA Loops (covered in the previous chapter), without a limit. If you are using Excel 2003, you can only nest loops seven times, but if you use Excel 2007, you can use 64. The latest versions of Excel allow a larger level of nesting.

Let us look at the following example:

Example 1

[14]

```
Sub ElseIfStructure()
'Returns Good if the marks are equal to 60.
Dim sngMarks As Single
sngMarks = 60
If sngMarks >= 80 Then
MsgBox "Excellent"
ElseIf sngMarks >= 60 And sngMarks < 80 Then
MsgBox "Good"
ElseIf sngMarks >= 40 And sngMarks < 60 Then
MsgBox "Average"
Else
MsgBox "Poor"
End If
End Sub
```

---

[14] Conditional Statements in Excel VBA - If, Case, For, Do Loops. (2019). Retrieved from https://analysistabs.com/excel-vba/conditional-statements/

Example 2

In this example, we will use Multiple If...Then Statements. This is an alternative to the ElseIf structure, but is not as efficient as the ElseIf Structure. In the Multiple If...Then Statements, the compiler will need to run through every If...Then block of code even after it returns the result true for one of the conditions. If you use the ElseIf structure, the subsequent conditions are not checked if one condition is true. This makes the ElseIf structure faster. If you can perform the function using the ElseIf structure, you should avoid using the Multiple If...Then Structure.

Sub multipleIfThenStmnts()

"Returns Good if the marks are equal to 60.

Dim sngMarks As Single

sngMarks = 60

If sngMarks >= 80 Then

MsgBox "Excellent"

End If

If sngMarks >= 60 And sngMarks < 80 Then

MsgBox "Good"

End If

If sngMarks >= 40 And sngMarks < 60 Then

MsgBox "Average"

End If

If sngMarks < 40 Then

MsgBox "Poor"

End If

End Sub

Example 3

In this example, we will nest the If...Then...Else statements within a For...Next Loop.

Sub IfThenNesting()

'The user will need to enter 5 numbers. The compiler will add the even numbers and subtract the odd numbers.

Dim i As Integer, n As Integer, iEvenSum As Integer, iOddSum As Integer

For n = 1 To 5

i = InputBox("enter number")

If i Mod 2 = 0 Then

iEvenSum = iEvenSum + i

Else

iOddSum = iOddSum + i

End If

Next n

MsgBox "sum of even numbers is " & iEvenSum

MsgBox "sum of odd numbers is " & iOddSum

End Sub

Example 4

You can use the following options to test multiple variables using the If...Then statements.

Option 1: ElseIf Structure

Sub IfThen1()

'this procedure returns the message "Pass in maths and Fail in science"

Dim sngMaths As Single, sngScience As Single

sngMaths = 50

sngScience = 30

If sngMaths >= 40 And sngScience >= 40 Then

MsgBox "Pass in both maths and science"

ElseIf sngMaths >= 40 And sngScience < 40 Then

MsgBox "Pass in maths and Fail in science"

ElseIf sngMaths < 40 And sngScience >= 40 Then

MsgBox "Fail in maths and Pass in science"

Else

MsgBox "Fail in both maths and science"

End If

End Sub

Option 2: If...Then...Else Nesting

Sub IfThen2()

'this procedure returns the message "Pass in maths and Fail in science"

Dim sngMaths As Single, sngScience As Single

sngMaths = 50

sngScience = 30

If sngMaths >= 40 Then

If sngScience >= 40 Then

MsgBox "Pass in both maths and science"

Else

MsgBox "Pass in maths and Fail in science"

End If

Else

If sngScience >= 40 Then

MsgBox "Fail in maths and Pass in science"

Else

MsgBox "Fail in both maths and science"

End If

End If

End Sub

Option 3: Multiple If...Then Statements

As mentioned earlier, this may not be the best way to perform the operation.

Sub IfThen3()

'this procedure returns the message "Pass in maths and Fail in science"

Dim sngMaths As Single, sngScience As Single

sngMaths = 50

sngScience = 30

If sngMaths >= 40 And sngScience >= 40 Then

MsgBox "Pass in both maths and science"

End If

If sngMaths >= 40 And sngScience < 40 Then

MsgBox "Pass in maths and Fail in science"

End If

If sngMaths < 40 And sngScience >= 40 Then

MsgBox "Fail in maths and Pass in science"

End If

If sngMaths < 40 And sngScience < 40 Then

MsgBox "Fail in both maths and science"

End If

End Sub

Example 5

In this example, we will use the If Not, If IsNumeric and IsEmpty functions in the Worksheet_Change event.

Private Sub Worksheet_Change(ByVal Target As Range)

'Using If IsEmpty, If Not and If IsNumeric (in If...Then statements) in the Worksheet_Change event.

'auto run a VBA code, when content of a worksheet cell changes, with the Worksheet_Change event.

On Error GoTo ErrHandler

Application.EnableEvents = False

'if target cell is empty post change, nothing will happen

If IsEmpty(Target) Then

Application.EnableEvents = True

Exit Sub

End If

'using If Not statement with the Intersect Method to determine if Target cell(s) is within specified range of "B1:B20"

If Not Intersect(Target, Range("B1:B20")) Is Nothing Then

'if target cell is changed to a numeric value

If IsNumeric(Target) Then

'changes the target cell color to yellow

Target.Interior.Color = RGB(255, 255, 0)

End If

End If

Application.EnableEvents = True

ErrHandler:

    Application.EnableEvents = True

    Exit Sub

End Sub

Using the Not Operator

When you use the Not operator on any Boolean expression, the compiler will reverse the true value with the false value and vice versa. The Not operator will always reverse the logic in any conditional statement. In the example above, If Not Intersect(Target, Range("B1:B20")) Is Nothing Then means If Intersect(Target, Range("B1:B20")) Is Not Nothing Then or If Intersect(Target, Range("B1:B20")) Is Something Then. In simple words, this means that the condition should not be true if the range falls or intersects between the range ("B1:B20").

Single Line If...Then...Else Statements

If you are writing a short or simple code, you should use the single-line syntax. If you wish to distinguish between the singly-line and multiple-line syntax, you should look at the block of code that succeeds the Then keyword. If there is nothing succeeding the Then keyword, the block of code is multiple-line. Otherwise, it is a single-line code.

The syntax for Single-line statements is as follows:

If condition Then statements Else else_statements

These blocks of statements can also be nested in one line by nesting the information within each conditional statement. You can insert the clause Else If in the code, which is similar to the ElseIf clause. You do not need to use the End If keywords in the single-syntax block of code since the program will automatically terminate.

Let us look at some examples[15] where we will use the single-line syntax for the If...Then...Else statements.

If sngMarks > 80 Then MsgBox "Excellent Marks"

If sngMarks > 80 Then MsgBox "Excellent Marks" Else MsgBox "Not Excellent"

'add MsgBox title "Grading":

If sngMarks > 80 Then MsgBox "Excellent Marks", , "Grading"

'using logical operator And in the condition:

If sngMarks > 80 And sngAvg > 80 Then MsgBox "Both Marks & Average are Excellent" Else MsgBox "Not Excellent"

'nesting another If...Then statement:

If sngMarks > 80 Then If sngAvg > 80 Then MsgBox "Both Marks & Average are Excellent"

---

[15] Conditional Statements in Excel VBA - If, Case, For, Do Loops. (2019). Retrieved from https://analysistabs.com/excel-vba/conditional-statements/

Example 1[16]

Sub IfThenSingleLine1()

Dim sngMarks As Single

sngMarks = 85

'Execute multiple statements / codes after Then keyword. Code will return 3 messages: "Excellent Marks - 85 on 90"; "Keep it up!" and "94.44% marks".

If sngMarks = 85 Then MsgBox "Excellent Marks - 85 on 90": MsgBox "Keep it up!": MsgBox Format(85 / 90 * 100, "0.00") & "% marks"

End Sub

Example 2

[17]Sub IfThenSingleLine1()

Dim sngMarks As Single

sngMarks = 85

'Execute multiple statements / codes after Then keyword. Code will return 3 messages: "Excellent Marks - 85 on 90"; "Keep it up!" and "94.44% marks".

---

[16] Conditional Statements in Excel VBA - If, Case, For, Do Loops. (2019). Retrieved from https://analysistabs.com/excel-vba/conditional-statements/

[17] Conditional Statements in Excel VBA - If, Case, For, Do Loops. (2019). Retrieved from https://analysistabs.com/excel-vba/conditional-statements/

If sngMarks = 85 Then MsgBox "Excellent Marks - 85 on 90": MsgBox "Keep it up!": MsgBox Format(85 / 90 * 100, "0.00") & "% marks"

End Sub

Example 3

[18]Sub IfThenSingleLine2()

Dim sngMarks As Single, sngAvg As Single

sngMarks = 85

sngAvg = 75

'nesting If...Then statements. Code will return the message: "Marks are Excellent, but Average is not"

If sngMarks > 80 Then If sngAvg > 80 Then MsgBox "Both Marks & Average are Excellent" Else MsgBox "Marks are Excellent, but Average is not" Else MsgBox "Marks are not Excellent"

End Sub

Example 4

[19]Sub IfThenSingleLine3()

Dim sngMarks As Single

sngMarks = 65

---

[18] Conditional Statements in Excel VBA - If, Case, For, Do Loops. (2019). Retrieved from https://analysistabs.com/excel-vba/conditional-statements/

[19] Conditional Statements in Excel VBA - If, Case, For, Do Loops. (2019). Retrieved from https://analysistabs.com/excel-vba/conditional-statements/

'using the keywords Else If (in single-line syntax), similar to ElseIf (in multiple-line syntax). Procedure will return the message: "Marks are Good".

If sngMarks > 80 Then MsgBox "Marks are Excellent" Else If sngMarks >= 60 Then MsgBox "Marks are Good" Else If sngMarks >= 40 Then MsgBox "Marks are Average" Else MsgBox "Marks are Poor"

End Sub

Select...Case Statement

The Select...Case statement will execute statements or a block of code depending on whether some conditions have been met. It will evaluate an expression and executes one of the many blocks of code depending on what the result is. This statement is similar to the If...The...Else statement.

Syntax

Select Case expression

Case expression_value_1

statements_1

Case expression_value_n

statements_n

Case Else

else_statements

End Select

Expression

This can be a range, field or a variable. The expression can be expressed by using a VBA function -> as "rng.HasFormula" or "IsNumeric(rng)" where the 'rng' is the range variable. The expression can return a String value, Boolean Value, Numeric Value or any other data type. It is important that you specify the expression. It is the value of the expression that the compiler will test and compare with each case in the Select...Case statement. When the values match, the compiler will execute the block of code under the matching Case.

Expression_value

The data type of the expression_value should be the same as the expression or a similar data type. The compiler will compare the value of the expression against the expression_value in each case. If it finds a match, the block of code under the case or the statements will be executed. You must specify at least one expression_value, and the compiler will test the expression against these values in the order they are mentioned in. The expression_values are similar to a list of conditions where the condition must be met for the relevant block of code to be executed.

Statements

The compiler will execute the block of code or statements under a specific case if the value of the expression and the expression_value are the same.

Case Else -> expression_value

When the compiler matches the value of the expression to the expression_value, it will execute the block of code under that case. It will not check the value of the expression against the remaining expression_value. If the compiler does not find a match against any expression_value, it will move to the Case Else clause. The statements under this clause are executed. You do not have to use this clause when you write your code.

Else_statements

As mentioned earlier, the else_statements are included in the Case Else section of the code. If the compiler cannot match the value of the expression to any expression_value, it will execute these statements.

End Select

These keywords[20] terminate the Select...Case block of statements. You must mention these keywords at the end of the Select...Case statements.

Let us look at an example of the Select...Case statements.

Sub selectCase1()

'making strAge equivalent to "young" will return the message "Less than 40 years"

Dim strAge As String

strAge = "young"

Select Case strAge

Case "senior citizen"

MsgBox "Over 60 years"

---

[20] Conditional Statements in Excel VBA - If, Case, For, Do Loops. (2019). Retrieved from https://analysistabs.com/excel-vba/conditional-statements/

Case "middle age"

MsgBox "Between 40 to 59 years"

Case "young"

MsgBox "Less than 40 years"

Case Else

MsgBox "Invalid"

End Select

End Sub

Using the To Keyword

You can use the To keyword to specify the upper and lower range of all matching values in the expression_value section of the Select...Case statements. The value on the left side of the To keyword should either be less than or equal to the value on the right side of the To keyword. You can also specify the range for a specified set of characters.

Let us look at an example[21].

Sub selectCaseTo()

'entering marks as 69 will return the message "Average"; entering marks as 101 will return the message "Out of Range"

Dim iMarks As Integer

iMarks = InputBox("Enter marks")

---

[21] Conditional Statements in Excel VBA - If, Case, For, Do Loops. (2019). Retrieved from https://analysistabs.com/excel-vba/conditional-statements/

```
Select Case iMarks

Case 70 To 100

MsgBox "Good"

Case 40 To 69

MsgBox "Average"

Case 0 To 39

MsgBox "Failed"

Case Else

MsgBox "Out of Range"

End Select

End Sub
```

Using the Is Keyword

You can use the Is keyword if you want to include a comparison operator like <>, =, <=, >=, < or >. If you do not include the Is keyword, the compiler will automatically include it. Let us look at the example[22] below.

```
Sub selectCaseIs()

'if sngTemp equals 39.5, returned message is "Moderately Hot"

Dim sngTemp As Single

sngTemp = 39.5
```

---

[22] Conditional Statements in Excel VBA - If, Case, For, Do Loops. (2019). Retrieved from https://analysistabs.com/excel-vba/conditional-statements/

Select Case sngTemp

Case Is >= 40

MsgBox "Extremely Hot"

Case Is >= 25

MsgBox "Moderately Hot"

Case Is >= 0

MsgBox "Cool Weather"

Case Is < 0

MsgBox "Extremely Cold"

End Select

End Sub

Using a comma

You can include multiple ranges or expressions in the Case clause. These ranges and expressions can be separated with a comma. The comma acts like the OR operator. You can also specify multiple expressions and ranges for character strings. Let us look at the example below.

Example 1

[23]Sub selectCaseMultiple_1()

'if alpha equates to "Hello", the returned message is "Odd Number or Hello"

Dim alpha As Variant

alpha = "Hello"

Select Case alpha

Case a, e, i, o, u

MsgBox "Vowels"

Case 2, 4, 6, 8

MsgBox "Even Number"

Case 1, 3, 5, 7, 9, "Hello"

MsgBox "Odd Number or Hello"

Case Else

MsgBox "Out of Range"

End Select

End Sub

---

[23] Conditional Statements in Excel VBA - If, Case, For, Do Loops. (2019). Retrieved from https://analysistabs.com/excel-vba/conditional-statements/

Example 2

[24]In this example, we are comparing the strings "apples" to "grapes." The compiler will determine the value between "apples" and "grapes" and will use the default comparison method binary.

Sub SelectCaseMultiple_OptionCompare_NotSpecified()

'Option Compare is NOT specified and therefore text comparison will be case-sensitive

'bananas will return the message "Text between apples and grapes, or specifically mangoes, or the numbers 98 or 99"; oranges will return the message "Out of Range"; Apples will return the message "Out of Range".

Dim var As Variant, strResult As String

var = InputBox("Enter")

Select Case var

Case 1 To 10, 11 To 20: strResult = "Number is between 1 and 20"

Case "apples" To "grapes", "mangoes", 98, 99: strResult = "Text between apples and grapes, or specifically mangoes, or the numbers 98 or 99"

Case Else: strResult = "Out of Range"

End Select

MsgBox strResult

End Sub

---

[24] Conditional Statements in Excel VBA - If, Case, For, Do Loops. (2019). Retrieved from https://analysistabs.com/excel-vba/conditional-statements/

Nesting

You can nest the Select...Case block of code or statements within VBA loops, If...Then...Else statements and within a Select...Case block. There is no limit on the number of cases you can include in the code. If you are nesting a Select...Case within another Select...Case, it should be a complete block by itself and also terminate with its End Select.

Example 1

[25]Sub selectCaseNested1()

'check if a range is empty; and if not empty, whether has a numeric value and if numeric then if also has a formula; and if not numeric then what is the text length.

Dim rng As Range, iLength As Integer

Set rng = ActiveSheet.Range("A1")

Select Case IsEmpty(rng)

Case True

MsgBox rng.Address & " is empty"

Case Else

Select Case IsNumeric(rng)

Case True

MsgBox rng.Address & " has a numeric value"

---

[25] Conditional Statements in Excel VBA - If, Case, For, Do Loops. (2019). Retrieved from https://analysistabs.com/excel-vba/conditional-statements/

Select Case rng.HasFormula

Case True

MsgBox rng.Address & " also has a formula"

End Select

Case Else

iLength = Len(rng)

MsgBox rng.Address & " has a Text length of " & iLength

End Select

End Select

End Sub

Example 2

[26]Function StringManipulation(str As String) As String

'This code customizes a string text as follows:

'1. removes numericals from a text string;

'2. removes leading, trailing & inbetween spaces (leaves single space between words);

'3. adds space (if not present) after each exclamation, comma, full stop and question mark;

---

[26] Conditional Statements in Excel VBA - If, Case, For, Do Loops. (2019). Retrieved from https://analysistabs.com/excel-vba/conditional-statements/

'4. capitalizes the very first letter of the string and the first letter of a word after each exclamation, full stop and question mark;

```
Dim iTxtLen As Integer, iStrLen As Integer, n As Integer, i As Integer, ansiCode As Integer
```

'---------------------------

'REMOVE NUMERICALS

'chr(48) to chr(57) represent numericals 0 to 9 in ANSI/ASCII character codes

```
For i = 48 To 57
```

'remove all numericals from the text string using vba Replace function:

```
str = Replace(str, Chr(i), "")

Next i
```

'---------------------------

'REMOVE LEADING, TRAILING & INBETWEEN SPACES (LEAVE SINGLE SPACE BETWEEN WORDS)

'use the worksheet TRIM function. Note: the TRIM function removes space character with ANSI code 32, does not remove the nonbreaking space character with ANSI code 160

```
str = Application.Trim(str)
```

'---------------------------

'ADD SPACE (IF NOT PRESENT) AFTER EACH EXCLAMATION, COMMA, DOT AND QUESTION MARK:

'set variable value to string length:

iTxtLen = Len(str)

For n = iTxtLen To 1 Step -1

'Chr(32) returns space; Chr(33) returns exclamation; Chr(44) returns comma; Chr(46) returns full stop; Chr(63) returns question mark;

If Mid(str, n, 1) = Chr(33) Or Mid(str, n, 1) = Chr(44) Or Mid(str, n, 1) = Chr(46) Or Mid(str, n, 1) = Chr(63) Then

'check if space is not present:

If Mid(str, n + 1, 1) <> Chr(32) Then

'using Mid & Right functions to add space - note that current string length is used:

str = Mid(str, 1, n) & Chr(32) & Right(str, iTxtLen - n)

'update string length - increments by 1 after adding a space (character):

iTxtLen = iTxtLen + 1

End If

End If

Next n

'DELETE SPACE (IF PRESENT) BEFORE EACH EXCLAMATION, COMMA, DOT & QUESTION MARK:

'reset variable value to string length:

iTxtLen = Len(str)

For n = iTxtLen To 1 Step -1

'Chr(32) returns space; Chr(33) returns exclamation; Chr(44) returns comma; Chr(46) returns full stop; Chr(63) returns question mark;

If Mid(str, n, 1) = Chr(33) Or Mid(str, n, 1) = Chr(44) Or Mid(str, n, 1) = Chr(46) Or Mid(str, n, 1) = Chr(63) Then

'check if space is present:

If Mid(str, n - 1, 1) = Chr(32) Then

'using the worksheet Replace function to delete a space:

str = Application.Replace(str, n - 1, 1, "")

'omit rechecking the same character again - position of n shifts (decreases by 1) due to deleting a space character:

n = n - 1

End If

End If

Next n

'----------------------------

'CAPITALIZE LETTERS:

'capitalize the very first letter of the string and the first letter of a word after each exclamation, full stop and question mark, while all other letters are lowercase

iStrLen = Len(str)

For i = 1 To iStrLen

'determine the ANSI code of each character in the string

ansiCode = Asc(Mid(str, i, 1))

Select Case ansiCode

'97 to 122 are the ANSI codes equating to small cap letters "a" to "z"

Case 97 To 122

If i > 2 Then

'capitalizes a letter whose position is 2 characters after (1 character after, will be the space character added earlier) an exclamation, full stop and question mark:

If Mid(str, i - 2, 1) = Chr(33) Or Mid(str, i - 2, 1) = Chr(46) Or Mid(str, i - 2, 1) = Chr(63) Then

Mid(str, i, 1) = UCase(Mid(str, i, 1))

End If

'capitalize first letter of the string:

ElseIf i = 1 Then

Mid(str, i, 1) = UCase(Mid(str, i, 1))

End If

'if capital letter, skip to next character (ie. next i):

Case Else

GoTo skip

End Select

skip:

Next i

'------------------------

'manipulated string:

StringManipulation = str

End Function

Sub Str_Man()

'specify text string to manipulate & get manipulated string

Dim strText As String

'specify the text string, which is required to be manipulated

strText = ActiveSheet.Range("A1").Value

'the manipulated text string is entered in range A5 of the active sheet, on running the procedure:

ActiveSheet.Range("A5").Value = StringManipulation(strText)

End Sub

Go To Statement

You can use the Go To statement to move to a different section of the code or jump a line in the procedure. There are two parts to the Go To statement:

1. The GoTo keywords that are followed by an identifier, also known as the Label.
2. The Label which is followed by a colon and the line of code or a few statements.

If the value of the expression satisfies the condition, the compiler will move to a separate line of code that is indicated in the GoTo statement. You can avoid this statement and use the If…Then…Else statement. The Go To function makes the code unreadable and confusing.

Select...Case Statements Versus the If...Then...Else Statements

The Select...Case and If...Then...Else statements are both conditional statements. In each of these statements either one or more conditions are tested and the compiler will execute the block of code depending on what the result of the evaluation is.

The difference between the two statements is that in the Select...Case statement only one condition is evaluated at a time. The variable that is to be evaluated is initialized or declared in the Select Case expression. The multiple case statements will specify the different values that the variable can take. In the If...Then...Else statement, multiple conditions can be evaluated and the code for different conditions can be executed at the same time.

The Select...Case statement will only test a single variable for several values while the If...Then...Else statement will test multiple variables for different values. In this sense, the If...Then... Else statement is more flexible since you can test multiple variables for different conditions.

If you are testing a large number of conditions, you should avoid using the If...Then...Else statements since they may appear confusing. These statements can also make it difficult for you to read the code.

CHAPTER 7

Working With Strings

A string is an integral part of VBA, and every programmer must work with strings if they want to automate functions in Excel using VBA. There are many manipulations that one can perform on a string including:

- Removing the blanks in a string

- Extracting some parts of a string

- Converting a number into a string

- Finding the characters in a string

- Formatting dates to include weekdays

- Parsing the string into an array

- Comparing different strings

VBA provides you with different functions that you can use to perform these tasks. This chapter will help you understand how you can work with different strings in VBA. This chapter leaves you with some simple examples that you can use for practice.

Points to Remember

You must keep the following points in mind when you want to work with strings.

Original String Does Not Change

When you perform any operation on a string, the original value of the string will never change. VBA will only return a new string with the necessary changes made. If you want to make changes to the original string, you must assign the result of the function to the original string to replace the original string. This concept is covered later in this chapter.

Comparing Two Strings

There are some string functions like Instr() and StrComp() that allow you to include the **Compare** parameter. This parameter works in the following way:

- **vbTextCompare**: The upper and lower case letters in the string are considered the same.

- **vbBinaryCompare**: The upper and lower case letters in the string are treated differently.

Let us look at the following example[27] to see how you can use the Compare parameter in the StrComp() function.

---

[27] String Manipulation in Excel VBA. (2019). Retrieved from https://www.excel-easy.com/vba/string-manipulation.html

```
Sub Comp1()
    ' Prints 0 if the strings do not match
    Debug.Print StrComp("MARoon", "Maroon", vbTextCompare)
    ' Prints 1 if the strings do not match
    Debug.Print StrComp("Maroon", "MAROON", vbBinaryCompare)
End Sub
```

Instead of using the same parameter every time, you can use the Option Compare. This parameter is defined at the top of any module, and a function that includes the parameter Compare will use this setting as its default. You can use the Option Compare in the following ways:

Option Compare Text

This option makes uses the vbTextCompare as the default compare argument.

Option Compare[28] Text

```
Sub Comp2()
    ' Strings match - uses vbCompareText as Compare argument
    Debug.Print StrComp("ABC", "abc")
    Debug.Print StrComp("DEF", "def")
End Sub
```

---

[28] String Manipulation in Excel VBA. (2019). Retrieved from https://www.excel-easy.com/vba/string-manipulation.html

Option Compare Binary

This option uses the vbBinaryCompare as the default compare argument.

Option Compare[29] Binary

Sub Comp2()

    ' Strings do not match - uses vbCompareBinary as Compare argument

    Debug.Print StrComp("ABC", "abc")

    Debug.Print StrComp("DEF", "def")

End Sub

If you do not use the Option Compare statement, VBA uses Option Compare Binary as the default. Please keep these points in mind when we look at the individual string functions.

Appending Strings

You can use the & operator to append strings in VBA. Let us look at some examples of how you can use this operator to append[30] strings.

Sub Append()

    Debug.Print "ABC" & "DEF"

    Debug.Print "Jane" & " " & "Smith"

---

[29] String Manipulation in Excel VBA. (2019). Retrieved from https://www.excel-easy.com/vba/string-manipulation.html

[30] String Manipulation in Excel VBA. (2019). Retrieved from https://www.excel-easy.com/vba/string-manipulation.html

        Debug.Print "Long " & 22

        Debug.Print "Double " & 14.99

        Debug.Print "Date " & #12/12/2015#

End Sub

In the example above, there are different types of data that we have converted to string using the quotes. You will see that the plus operator can also be used to append strings in some programs. The difference between using the & operator and + operator is that the latter will only work with string data types. If you use it with any other data type, you will get an error message.

        ' You will get the following error: "Type Mismatch"

        Debug.Print "Long " + 22

If you want to use a complex function to append strings, you should use the Format function which is described later in this chapter.

Extracting Parts of a String

In this section, we will look at some functions that you can use to extract information or data from strings.

You can use the Right, Left and Mid functions to extract the necessary parts in a string. These functions[31] are simple to use. The Right function reads the sentence from the right, the Left function reads the sentence from the left and the Mid function will read the sentence from the point that you specify.

---

[31] String Manipulation in Excel VBA. (2019). Retrieved from https://www.excel-easy.com/vba/string-manipulation.html

```
Sub UseLeftRightMid()

    Dim sCustomer As String

    sCustomer = "John Thomas Smith"

    Debug.Print Left(sCustomer, 4)  ' This will print John

    Debug.Print Right(sCustomer, 5) ' This will print Smith

    Debug.Print Left(sCustomer, 11)  ' This will print John Thomas

    Debug.Print Right(sCustomer, 12) ' This will print Thomas Smith

    Debug.Print Mid(sCustomer, 1, 4) ' This will print John

    Debug.Print Mid(sCustomer, 6, 6) ' This will print Thomas

    Debug.Print Mid(sCustomer, 13, 5) ' This will print Smith

End Sub[32]
```

As mentioned earlier, the string functions in VBA do not change the original string but return a new string as the result. In the following example, you will see that the string "FullName" remains unchanged even after the use of the Left function.

---

[32] String Manipulation in Excel VBA. (2019). Retrieved from https://www.excel-easy.com/vba/string-manipulation.html

```
Sub UsingLeftExample()
    Dim Fullname As String
    Fullname = "John Smith"
    Debug.Print "Firstname is: "; Left(Fullname, 4)
    ' The original string remains unchanged
    Debug.Print "Fullname is: "; Fullname
End Sub
```

If you wish to make a change to the original string, you will need to assign the return value of the function to the original string.

```
Sub ChangingString()
    Dim name As String
    name = "John Smith"
    ' The return value of the function is assigned to the original string
    name = Left(name, 4)
    Debug.Print "Name is: "; name
End Sub
```

Searching in a String

InStr and InStrRev are two functions that you can use in VBA to search for substrings within a string. If the compiler can find the substring in the string, the position of the string is returned. This position is the index from where the string starts. If the substring is not found, the compiler will return zero. If the original string and substring are null, the value null is returned.

InStr

Description of Parameters

The function is written[33] as follows:

InStr() Start[Optional], String1, String2, Compare[Optional]

1. **Start**: This number specified where the compiler should start looking for the substring within the actual string. The default option is one.

2. **String1**: This is the original string.

3. **String2**: This is the substring that you want the compiler to search for.

4. **Compare**: This is the method we looked at in the first part of this chapter.

The Use and Examples

This function will return the first position in the string where the substring is found. Let us look at the following example:

Sub FindSubString()

  Dim name As String

    name = "John Smith"

---

[33] String Manipulation in Excel VBA. (2019). Retrieved from https://www.excel-easy.com/vba/string-manipulation.html

' This will return the number 3 which indicates the position of the first h

Debug.Print InStr(name, "h")

' This will return the number 10 which indicates the position of the first h starting from position 4

Debug.Print InStr(4, name, "h")

' This will return 8

Debug.Print InStr(name, "it")

' This will return 6

Debug.Print InStr(name, "Smith")

' This will return zero since the string "SSS" was not found

Debug.Print InStr(name, "SSS")

End Sub

InStrRev

Description of Parameters

The function is written as follows:

InStrRev() StringCheck, StringMatch, Start[Optional], Compare[Optional]

1. **StringCheck**: This is the string that you need to search for.
2. **StringMatch**: This is the string the compiler should look for.
3. **Start**: This number specified where the compiler should start looking for the substring within the actual string. The default option is one.

4. **Compare**: This is the method we looked at in the first part of this chapter.

The Use and Examples

This function is the same as the InStr function except that is starts the search from the end of the original string. You must note that the position that the compiler returns is the position from the start of the sentence. Therefore, if the substring is available only once in the sentence, the InStr() and InStrRev() functions return the same value.

Let us look at some examples[34] of the InStrRev function.

Sub UsingInstrRev()

    Dim name As String

    name = "John Smith"

    ' Both functions will return 1 which is the position of the only J

    Debug.Print InStr(name, "J")

    Debug.Print InStrRev(name, "J")

    ' This will return 10 which indicates the second h

    Debug.Print InStrRev(name, "h")

    ' This will return the number 3 and it indicates the first h as searches from position

    Debug.Print InStrRev(name, "h", 9)

    ' This will return 1

---

[34] String Manipulation in Excel VBA. (2019). Retrieved from https://www.excel-easy.com/vba/string-manipulation.html

```
Debug.Print InStrRev(name, "John")
```

End Sub

You should use the InStr and InStrRev functions when you want to perform basic searches in strings. If you want to extract some text from a string, the process is slightly complicated.

Removing Blanks

In VBA, you can use the trim functions to remove blanks or spaces either at the start or end of a string.

The Use and Examples

1. [35]**Trim**: Removes the spaces from both the right and left of a string.

2. **LTrim**: Removes the spaces only from the left of the string.

3. **RTrim**: Removes the spaces from the right of the string.

```
Sub TrimStr()

    Dim name As String

    name = " John Smith  "

    ' Will print "John Smith  "

    Debug.Print LTrim(name)

    ' Will print "  John Smith"

    Debug.Print RTrim(name)

    ' Will print "John Smith"
```

---

[35] String Manipulation in Excel VBA. (2019). Retrieved from https://www.excel-easy.com/vba/string-manipulation.html

Debug.Print Trim(name)

End Sub

Length of a String[36]

You can use Len to return the length of the string. This function will only return the number of characters in the string. You can use different data types if you want to identify the number of bytes in the string.

Sub GetLen()

    Dim name As String

    name = "John Smith"

    ' This will print 10

    Debug.Print Len("John Smith")

    ' This will print 3

    Debug.Print Len("ABC")

    ' This will print 4 since the numeric data type Long is 4 bytes in size

    Dim total As Long

    Debug.Print Len(total)

End Sub

---

[36] String Manipulation in Excel VBA. (2019). Retrieved from https://www.excel-easy.com/vba/string-manipulation.html

Reversing a String[37]

If you want to reverse the characters in the original string, you can use the StrReverse function. This functions is extremely easy to use.

Sub RevStr()

    Dim s As String

    s = "Jane Smith"

    ' This will print htimS enaJ

    Debug.Print StrReverse(s)

End Sub

Comparing Strings

You can use the function StrComp to compare two strings.

Description of Parameters

The function is written as follows:

StrComp() String1, String2, Compare[Optional]

1. **String1**: The first string that needs to be compared.
2. **String2**: The second string that needs to be compared.
3. **Compare**: This is the method we looked at in the first part of this chapter.

---

[37] String Manipulation in Excel VBA. (2019). Retrieved from https://www.excel-easy.com/vba/string-manipulation.html

The Use and Examples[38]

Let us look at some examples of how to use the StrComp function:

```
Sub UsingStrComp()
  ' This will return 0
  Debug.Print StrComp("ABC", "ABC", vbTextCompare)
  ' This will return 1
  Debug.Print StrComp("ABCD", "ABC", vbTextCompare)
  ' This will return -1
  Debug.Print StrComp("ABC", "ABCD", vbTextCompare)
  ' This will return Null
  Debug.Print StrComp(Null, "ABCD", vbTextCompare)
End Sub
```

Comparing Strings Using Operators

You can use the equal to sign to compare two strings in VBA. The differences between the equal to sign and the StrComp function are:

- The former will only return true or false
- You cannot combine a Compare parameter with the equal sign since it will only use the Option Compare setting.

---

[38] String Manipulation in Excel VBA. (2019). Retrieved from https://www.excel-easy.com/vba/string-manipulation.html

Let us look at a few examples[39] where we use the equal to sign to compare two strings.

Option Compare Text

Sub CompareUsingEquals()

  ' This will return true

    Debug.Print "ABC" = "ABC"

    ' This will return True since the compare text parameter is at the start of the program

    Debug.Print "ABC" = "abc"

    ' This will return false

    Debug.Print "ABCD" = "ABC"

    ' This will return false

    Debug.Print "ABC" = "ABCD"

    ' This will return null

    Debug.Print Null = "ABCD"

End Sub

[40]To see if two strings are not equal, you must use the "<>" operator. This operator performs a function that is opposite to the equal to sign.

---

[39] String Manipulation in Excel VBA. (2019). Retrieved from https://www.excel-easy.com/vba/string-manipulation.html

Option Compare Text

Sub CompareWithNotEqual()

   ' This will return false

   Debug.Print "ABC" <> "ABC"

   ' This will return false since the Compare Text parameter is at the start of the program

   Debug.Print "ABC" <> "abc"

   ' This will return true

   Debug.Print "ABCD" <> "ABC"

   ' This will return true

   Debug.Print "ABC" <> "ABCD"

   ' This will return null

   Debug.Print Null <> "ABCD"

End Sub

Comparing Strings Using Pattern Matching

Pattern matching is a technique in VBA that allows you to determine if there is a specific pattern of characters used in a string. For example, there are some times when you will need to check if a specific value has three alphabetic and three numeric characters or if a string is followed by a set of characters or numbers. If the compiler

---

[40] String Manipulation in Excel VBA. (2019). Retrieved from https://www.excel-easy.com/vba/string-manipulation.html

deems that the string follows the specific pattern that you described, it will return "True," otherwise it will return "False."

The process of pattern matching is similar to the format function. This means that you can use the pattern matching process in many ways. In this section, we will look at a few examples which will help you understand how this technique works. Let us take the following string as an example[41]: [abc][!def]]?#X*

Let us look at how this string will work:

1. [abc]: This will represent a character – a, b or c.

2. [!def]: This will represent a character that is not d, e or f.

3. ?: This will represent any character.

4. #: This will represent any digit.

5. X: This represents the character X.

6. *: This means that the string is followed by more characters or zero.

Therefore, this is a valid string.

Now, let us consider the following string: apY6X.

1. a: This character is one of a, b and c.

2. p: This is not a character that is d, e or f.

3. Y: This is any character.

4. 6: This is a digit.

---

[41] String Manipulation in Excel VBA. (2019). Retrieved from https://www.excel-easy.com/vba/string-manipulation.html

5. X: This is the letter X.

You can now say that the pattern for both strings is the same.

Let us look at a code that will show you a variety of results when you use the same pattern:

Sub Patterns()

```
' This will print true
Debug.Print 1; "apY6X" Like "[abc][!def]?#X*"
' This will print true since any combination is valid after X
Debug.Print 2; "apY6Xsf34FAD" Like "[abc][!def]?#X*"
' This will print false since the character is not a, b or c
Debug.Print 3; "dpY6X" Like "[abc][!def]?#X*"
' This will print false since the character is one of d, e and f
Debug.Print 4; "aeY6X" Like "[abc][!def]?#X*"
' This will print false since the character at 4 should be a digit.
Debug.Print 5; "apYAX" Like "[abc][!def]?#X*"
' This will print false since the character at position 5 should be X.
Debug.Print 1; "apY6Z" Like "[abc][!def]?#X*"
```

End Sub

Replacing Part of a String

If you want to replace a substring in a string with another string, you should use the replace function. This function will allow you to replace all the instances in a string where the substring is found.

Description of Parameters

The function is written as follows:

Replace() Expression, Find, Replace, Start[Optional], Count[Optional], Compare[Optional]

1. Expression: This is the original string.

2. Find: This is the substring that you want to replace in the Expression string.

3. Replace: This is the substring you want to replace the Find substring with.

4. Start: This is the start position of the string. The position is taken as 1 by default.

5. Count: This is the number of substitutions you want to make. The default is one, which means that all the Find substrings are replaced with the Replace substring.

6. Compare: This is the method we looked at in the first part of this chapter.

The Use and Examples

In the following code, we will look at some examples of how to use the Replace function.

Sub ReplaceExamples()

' To replace all the question marks in the string with semicolons.

Debug.Print Replace("A?B?C?D?E", "?", ";")

' To replace Smith with Jones

Debug.Print Replace("Peter Smith,Ann Smith", "Smith", "Jones")

' To replace AX with AB

Debug.Print Replace("ACD AXC BAX", "AX", "AB")

End Sub

The output will be as follows:

A;B;C;D;E

Peter Jones,Sophia Jones

ACD ABC BAB

In the block of code below, we are using the Count optional parameter to determine the number of substitutions you want to make. For example, if you set the parameter equal to one, you are asking the compiler to replace the first occurrence that is found in the 'Find String' section.

```vb
Sub ReplaceCount()
    ' To replace only the first question mark
    Debug.Print Replace("A?B?C?D?E", "?", ";", Count:=1)
    ' To replace the first two question marks
    Debug.Print Replace("A?B?C?D?E", "?", ";", Count:=2)
End Sub
```

The output will be as follows:

A;B?C?D?E

A;B;C?D?E

If you use the Start optional parameter in the code, you can return only a part of the string. Based on the position that you mention in the Start parameter, the compiler will return the part of the string after that position. When you use this operator, the compiler will ignore the string before the specified start position.

```vb
Sub ReplacePartial()
    ' This will use the original string from the position 4
    Debug.Print Replace("A?B?C?D?E", "?", ";", Start:=4)
    ' This will use the original string from the position 8
    Debug.Print Replace("AA?B?C?D?E", "?", ";", Start:=8)
    ' There are no items that will be replaced, but it will return the last two values
    Debug.Print Replace("ABCD", "X", "Y", Start:=3)
End Sub
```

The output will be as follows:

;C;D;E

;E

CD

You may want to replace a lower case or upper case letter in a string, and to do this you can use the Compare parameter. This parameter can be used in different functions. If you want to learn more about this parameter, please read the section above.

Sub ReplaceCase()

    ' This will only replace the capitalized A's

    Debug.Print Replace("AaAa", "A", "X", Compare:=vbBinaryCompare)

    ' This will replace all the A's

    Debug.Print Replace("AaAa", "A", "X", Compare:=vbTextCompare)

End Sub

The output is as follows:

XaXa

XXXX

Multiple Replaces

You can also choose to nest the cells that you would like to replace with more than on string. Let us look at the example[42] below where we will need to replace X and Y with A and B respectively.

Sub ReplaceMulti()

    Dim newString As String

    ' Replace the A with X

    newString = Replace("ABCD ABDN", "A", "X")

    ' Replace the B with Y in the new string

    newString = Replace(newString, "B", "Y")

    Debug.Print newString

End Sub

In the example below, we will make some changes to the above code to perform this task. The value that is returned after the first function will be used as an argument or it could be used as the string for replacement.

---

[42] String Manipulation in Excel VBA. (2019). Retrieved from https://www.excel-easy.com/vba/string-manipulation.html

```
Sub ReplaceMultiNested()

    Dim newString As String

    ' To replace A with X and B with Y

    newString = Replace(Replace("ABCD ABDN", "A", "X"), "B", "Y")

    Debug.Print newString

End Sub
```

The result of these replacements will be XYCD XYDN.

CHAPTER 8

Arrays

You can use an array to store multiple items in a single container or variable, and use that container in your program. An array is analogous to a large box with a finite or infinite number of smaller boxes inside it. Each box will store a value depending on the data type of the array. You can also choose the number of small boxes you want to store data in. Remember that you can use an array only when you want to store items that have the same data type.

Structured Storage

An array is a list of items that have the same data type. One example of an array can be a to-do list that you prepare. The paper that contains the list of your tasks will form the single container, and this container holds numerous strings, and every string will list the tasks that you need to perform. You can also create the same paper in VBA using an array. An array can be defined using numerous techniques, and each of these techniques will use a similar approach.

Example

[43]' Tell VBA to start all arrays at 0.

Option Base 0

Public Sub SingleDimension()

' Define an output string.

Dim Output As String

' Define a variant to hold individual strings.

Dim IndividualString As Variant

' Define the array of strings.

Dim StringArray(5) As String

' Fill each array element with information.

StringArray(0) = "This"

StringArray(1) = "Is"

StringArray(2) = "An"

StringArray(3) = "Array"

StringArray(4) = "Of"

StringArray(5) = "Strings"

' Use the For Each...Next statement to get each array

---

[43] Kelly, P. (2019). The Complete Guide to Using Arrays in Excel VBA - Excel Macro Mastery. Retrieved from https://excelmacromastery.com/excel-vba-array/

' element and place it in a string.

For Each IndividualString In StringArray

' Create a single output string with the array

' array elements.

Output = Output + IndividualString + " "

Next

' Display the result.

MsgBox Trim(Output), _

vbInformation Or vbOKOnly, _

"Array Content"

End Sub

If you look at the code above, you will notice that it starts with the statement "Option Base 0." This statement will let VBA know that it should count the elements in the array starting with zero. The default setting is that VBA will count the elements in the array from zero. Most programming languages use zero as the starting point, and it is for this reason that the default for VBA is zero. Most of the older versions of VBA begin counting the elements in the array using 1 as the starting point.

If you want to use the code that you write in different environments, you should always include the Option Base statement. Since an array always starts at zero, and not one, you can store six elements although you define that the array should have five elements. The number that you include in the declaration does not define the number of elements in the array.

Array Types

An array can be classified into different types and this can be done using different methods. An array can be classified into different types depending on the data type of the elements in the array. An integer array is very different from a string array, and you can be certain that the elements in the array are distinct. You can use the Variant data type if you want to mix the data types in the array. Ensure that you are careful about using this data type since it can lead to some errors which will can be difficult for you to debug.

You can also define dimensions in an array which will define the directions in which the array can be allowed to hold any information. You can have a single-dimensional array, a two-dimensional array or an n-dimensional array, where n stands for a number.

Example: Adding an Element to an Array

Dim a As Range

Dim arr As Variant 'Just a Variant variable (i.e. don't pre-define it as an array)

For Each a In Range.Cells

    If IsEmpty(arr) Then

    arr = Array(a.value) 'Make the Variant an array with a single element

    Else

    ReDim Preserve arr(UBound(arr) + 1) 'Add next array element

    arr(UBound(arr)) = a.value   'Assign the array element

    End If

Next

VBA Array

In this section, we will look at the steps you need to follow to create an array.

Step 1 – Create A New Workbook

1. Open Microsoft Excel.

2. Save the excel workbook with the extension .xlsm

Step 2 – Add A Command Button

Now that you are familiar with creating an interface in a workbook. The previous chapters in the book will help you gather more information about the subroutines or subs and functions in VBA.

1. Add a command button to the active worksheet.

2. Set the property name to cmdLoadBeverages.

3. Now, set the Caption Property as Load Beverages.

The interface should now display the following:

Step 3 – Save The File

1. Now, save the file in the macro-enabled form of Excel.

Step 4 – Write The Code

The next step is to write the code for the application that you have developed:

1. You can view the code by right-clicking on the button.
2. Now, add the code below in the code window.

```
Private Sub cmdLoadBeverages_Click()

    Dim Drinks(1 To 4) As String

    Drinks(1) = "Pepsi"

    Drinks(2) = "Coke"

    Drinks(3) = "Fanta"

    Drinks(4) = "Juice"

    Sheet1.Cells(1, 1).Value = "My Favorite Beverages"

    Sheet1.Cells(2, 1).Value = Drinks(1)

    Sheet1.Cells(3, 1).Value = Drinks(2)

    Sheet1.Cells(4, 1).Value = Drinks(3)

    Sheet1.Cells(5, 1).Value = Drinks(4)

End Sub
```

Example To Enter Student Marks

Without An Array

In the example below, we will look at how you can enter the marks for every student without using an array.

```
Public Sub StudentMarks()
    With ThisWorkbook.Worksheets("Sheet1")
    ' Declare variable for each student
    Dim Student1 As Integer
    Dim Student2 As Integer
    Dim Student3 As Integer
    Dim Student4 As Integer
    Dim Student5 As Integer
    ' Read student marks from cell
    Student1 = .Range("C2").Offset(1)
    Student2 = .Range("C2") Offset(2)
    Student3 = .Range("C2").Offset(3)
    Student4 = .Range("C2").Offset(4)
    Student5 = .Range("C2").Offset(5)
    ' Print student marks
    Debug.Print "Students Marks"
    Debug.Print Student1
    Debug.Print Student2
    Debug.Print Student3
    Debug.Print Student4
    Debug.Print Student5
    End With
End Sub
```

The output will be the following,

Using An Array

Public Sub StudentMarksArr()

    With ThisWorkbook.Worksheets("Sheet1")

    ' Declare an array to hold marks for 5 students

    Dim Students(1 To 5) As Integer

    ' Read student marks from cells C3:C7 into array

    Dim i As Integer

    For i = 1 To 5

    Students(i) = .Range("C2").Offset(i)

    Next i

    ' Print student marks from the array

    Debug.Print "Students Marks"

    For i = LBound(Students) To UBound(Students)

    Debug.Print Students(i)

    Next i

    End With

End Sub

Notice the difference in the variables used in the two programs, and also notice the length of the program.

Example With Loops

[44]Public Sub ArrayLoops()

```
' Declare array
Dim arrMarks(0 To 5) As Long
' Fill the array with random numbers
Dim i As Long
For i = LBound(arrMarks) To UBound(arrMarks)
arrMarks(i) = 5 * Rnd
Next i
' Print out the values in the array
Debug.Print "Location", "Value"
For i = LBound(arrMarks) To UBound(arrMarks)
Debug.Print i, arrMarks(i)
Next i
End Sub
```

---

[44] Kelly, P. (2019). The Complete Guide to Using Arrays in Excel VBA - Excel Macro Mastery. Retrieved from https://excelmacromastery.com/excel-vba-array/

Sorting An Array

```
Sub QuickSort(arr As Variant, first As Long, last As Long)
  Dim vCentreVal As Variant, vTemp As Variant
  Dim lTempLow As Long
  Dim lTempHi As Long
  lTempLow = first
  lTempHi = last
  vCentreVal = arr((first + last) \ 2)
  Do While lTempLow <= lTempHi
        Do While arr(lTempLow) < vCentreVal And lTempLow < last
        lTempLow = lTempLow + 1
        Loop
        Do While vCentreVal < arr(lTempHi) And lTempHi > first
        lTempHi = lTempHi - 1
        Loop
        If lTempLow <= lTempHi Then
        ' Swap values
        vTemp = arr(lTempLow)
        arr(lTempLow) = arr(lTempHi)
        arr(lTempHi) = vTemp
```

```
    ' Move to next positions
    lTempLow = lTempLow + 1
    lTempHi = lTempHi - 1
    End If
    Loop
    If first < lTempHi Then QuickSort arr, first, lTempHi
    If lTempLow < last Then QuickSort arr, lTempLow, last
End Sub
```

Example For Creating A Two-Dimensional Array

[45]Public Sub TwoDimArray()

```
    ' Declare a two dimensional array
    Dim arrMarks(0 To 3, 0 To 2) As String
    ' Fill the array with text made up of i and j values
    Dim i As Long, j As Long
    For i = LBound(arrMarks) To UBound(arrMarks)
    For j = LBound(arrMarks, 2) To UBound(arrMarks, 2)
    arrMarks(i, j) = CStr(i) & ":" & CStr(j)
    Next j
```

---

[45] Kelly, P. (2019). The Complete Guide to Using Arrays in Excel VBA - Excel Macro Mastery. Retrieved from https://excelmacromastery.com/excel-vba-array/

Next i

' Print the values in the array to the Immediate Window

Debug.Print "i", "j", "Value"

For i = LBound(arrMarks) To UBound(arrMarks)

For j = LBound(arrMarks, 2) To UBound(arrMarks, 2)

Debug.Print i, j, arrMarks(i, j)

Next j

Next i

End Sub

CHAPTER 9

Error Handling And Debugging

Error handling is a common practice that every programmer uses to anticipate any error conditions that may arise when the program is run, and also include a few statements in the code. There are three types of errors that one can come across: run time errors that occur when the VBA editor cannot execute a specific statement in the code; compiler errors where a required variable has not been detected; and user entry data errors where the user does not enter the right type of information. This chapter will focus on run time errors since those errors are difficult to solve. The other two types are easy for the user to identify and correct. One of the most typical run time errors includes the one where the VBA editor is trying to access a workbook or worksheet that does not exist or is dividing a number by zero. The example being used in this chapter is trying to divide a number by zero.

It is important to include as many checks as possible when you write a program since that will help you ensure that there will be no run time errors when you write the code. This means that you should always ensure that every workbook or worksheet that you refer to in your code is present. You must also ensure that you are using the right name. When you check the application while writing the code, you can ensure that you avoid these silly mistakes. It is always good to detect the error while writing the code, and not when the application runs.

If you have written the code well, but still get a run time error and do not have any code written to handle those errors, VBA will display the error in a dialog box. When you are still building the application, you can welcome these errors. You cannot, however, be okay with receiving these errors when the application is being tested or is in the production environment. An error handling code will identify the error and correct that error immediately. The goal behind including an error handling code is to prevent the occurrence of any unhandled errors.

In this chapter, we will refer to the Property Procedure, Function and Sub as procedures and Exit Function, Exit Sub and Exit Property as an exit statement. End Function, End Sub, End and End Property will be represented by the words 'end statement.'

The On Error Statement

The On Error statement is at the heart of an error handling process. If a run time error occurs, this statement will instruct VBA to ignore the error and move on. There are three forms for the On Error statement:

1. On Error Goto 0

2. On Error Resume Next

3. On Error Goto <label>:

On Error Goto 0 is the default in VBA. This statement will indicate to VBA that it should always display the run time error in a dialog box if there is an error in the program. This will give you a chance to enter the debug mode and check the code. You can also choose to terminate the code. The On Error Goto 0 is the same as not including an error handling statement in your code. The error will prompt VBA to display the standard window.

The On Error Resume Next is one statement that most programmers misuse. This statement will instruct VBA to ignore the line of code with the error and move to the next line. Remember that this does not fix your code in any way, but will only tell VBA to act as if there was no error in the code. This will have a negative effect on the code. Therefore, it is important that you test your code for any errors and then fix them using appropriate methods. For the code below, you can fix the error by executing the program depending on whether the value of the variable Err.Number is zero or not.

>On Error Resume Next
>
>N = 1 / 0   ' cause an error
>
>If Err.Number <> 0 Then
>
>N = 1
>
>End If

In the code above, the value 1/0 is being assigned to the variable N. This approach is incorrect since VBA will give you the Division by Zero Error (Error 11). Since you have the On Error Resume Next statement, the code will continue to run. The statement will then assign a different value to the variable N once it tests the value for Err.Number.

The third form is the On Error Goto <label>. This line will let VBA know that it will need to execute a specific line of code or the line of code that is present immediately after a specific line label when an error occurs. Once the error occurs, VBA will ignore all the code between the specified line label and the error line.

```
On Error Goto ErrHandler:
N = 1 / 0        ' cause an error
'
' more code
'
Exit Sub
ErrHandler:
' error handling code
Resume Next
End Sub
```

Enabled And Active Error Handlers

VBA will create an error handler when the On Error statement is executed. You must remember that VBA can only activate the error handler block of code at a specific point, and behave according to the comments given in that block. If there are any errors, VBA will execute the code in the error handler block. Based on the On Error Goto <label> statement, VBA will execute the code provided in that location. The error handler block of code should either fix the error in the program or resume the execution of the main program. The error handler can also be used to terminate the program. You should not use it to skip a few lines of code. For instance, the code below will not function correctly:

```
On Error GoTo Err1:
Debug.Print 1 / 0
' more code
```

Err1:

    On Error GoTo Err2:

    Debug.Print 1 / 0

    ' more code

When the first error occurs, the execution of the code will be transferred to the block of code under Err1. The On Error statement will not identify the error since the error handler is active when the next error comes.

The Resume Statement

You can use the Resume statement to let VBA know that it should resume the execution of any code at a specific point or line in the code. Remember that you can use this statement only when you have an error handling code block. Do not use the Goto statement to tell VBA where it needs to go to execute the error handling code since this will lead to some issues.

There are three syntactic forms that the Resume statement takes:

1. Resume
2. Resume Next
3. Resume <label>

When you use the first form of the Resume statement, you will be instructing VBA to resume the execution of the program from the line that has the code. When you do this, you should ensure that the error handling code can fix the issue. Otherwise, the code will enter a loop since it will constantly jump between the line that has the error and the error handling code. In the example below, we will try to activate a worksheet that does not exist. You will receive the following error when you do this: "Subscript Out of Range." The compiler will then jump to the error handling code, and this code will create a sheet that will solve the problem.

    On Error GoTo ErrHandler:

    Worksheets("NewSheet").Activate

    Exit Sub

    ErrHandler:

    If Err.Number = 9 Then

    ' sheet does not exist, so create it

    Worksheets.Add.Name = "NewSheet"

    ' go back to the line of code that caused the problem

    Resume

    End If

The second form of the Resume method is Resume Next. This statement will let VBA know that it should execute the line of code that comes immediately after the line that gave rise to the error. The code below will set a value to the variable N, and this gives rise to an error. The error handling code will then assign the value 1 to the variable which will allow VBA to execute the rest of the program.

    On Error GoTo ErrHandler:

    N = 1 / 0

    Debug.Print N

    Exit Sub

    ErrHandler:

N = 1

' Move to the line that is immediately after the error

Resume Next

The third form of the Resume statement is Resume <label> form. This type of similar to the On Error Goto <label> statement. The former statement will tell VBA to execute the program from the line label. This means that it will avoid looking at the section of the code where there is an error. For example,

On Error GoTo ErrHandler:

N = 1 / 0

'

' This section contains the block of statements that will be skipped if there is an error

'

Label1:

'

' more code to execute

'

Exit Sub

ErrHandler:

' go back to the line at Label1:

Resume Label1:

An error object can either be reset or cleared using any form of the Resume statement.

Error Handling With Multiple Procedures

There is no need to include the error code in all procedures. VBA will always use the last On Error statement and act accordingly if there is any error in the program. The error is handled in the method mentioned above if the code causing the error is present in the same procedure as the last On Error statement. If there is no error handling code in the program, VBA will work backward and reach the incorrect section in the code. For example, a procedure A calls B and B calls C, and only procedure A has an error handling code. If an error occurs in C, VBA will go back to the error handling code in procedure A. It will skip all the code in procedure B.

A Note Of Caution

When you deal with errors, you may want to use the On Error Resume Next statement. This is a bad way to build a program since it is essential that you solve any error that you may come across. You must remember that this statement does not skip an error, but ignores it.

CHAPTER 10

How To Improve
The Performance Of Macros

There are times when VBA will run very slowly, and this is certainly frustrating. The good news is that there are some steps that you can take to improve the performance of the macro. This chapter will provide some information on the different steps you should take to improve the speed and performance of a macro. Regardless of whether you are an IT administrator, end user or a developer, you can use these tips to your benefit.

Close Everything Except For The VBA Essentials

The first thing to do to improve the performance of VBA is to turn off all the unnecessary features like screen updating, animation, automatic events and calculations when the macro runs. All these features will always add an extra overhead which will slow the macro down. This always happens when the macro needs to modify or change many cells and trigger a lot of recalculations or screen updates.

The code below will show you how you can enable or disable the following:

- Animations
- Screen updates
- Manual Calculations

```
Option Explicit

Dim lCalcSave As Long

Dim bScreenUpdate As Boolean

Sub SwitchOff(bSwitchOff As Boolean)

  Dim ws As Worksheet

  With Application

      If bSwitchOff Then

      ' OFF

      lCalcSave = .Calculation

      bScreenUpdate = .ScreenUpdating

      .Calculation = xlCalculationManual

      .ScreenUpdating = False

      .EnableAnimations = False

      '

      ' switch off display pagebreaks for all worksheets

      '
```

```
        For Each ws In ActiveWorkbook.Worksheets

            ws.DisplayPageBreaks = False

        Next ws

        Else

        ' ON

        If .Calculation <> lCalcSave And lCalcSave <> 0 Then .Calculation = lCalcSave

        .ScreenUpdating = bScreenUpdate

        .EnableAnimations = True

    End If

   End With

End Sub

Sub Main()

   SwitchOff(True) ' turn off these features

   MyFunction() ' do your processing here

   SwitchOff(False) ' turn these features back on

End Sub
```

Disabling All The Animations Using System Settings

You can disable animations through the Ease of Access center in Windows. You can use this center to disable some specific features in Excel by going to the Ease of Access or Advanced Tabs on the menu. For more information, please use the following link:

https://support.office.com/en-us/article/turn-off-office-animations-9ee5c4d2-d144-4fd2-b670-22cef9fa

Disabling Office Animations Using Registry Settings

You can always disable office animations on different computers by changing the appropriate registry key using a group policy setting.

HIVE: HKEY_CURRENT_USER

Key Path: Software\Microsoft\Office\16.0\Common\Graphics

Key Name: DisableAnimations

Value type: REG_DWORD

Value data: 0x00000001 (1)

If you use the Registry Editor incorrectly, you can cause some serious problems across the system. You may need to reinstall Windows to use the editor correctly. Microsoft will help you solve the problems of a Registry Editor, but you should use this tool if you are willing to take the risk.

Removing Unnecessary Selects

Most people use the select method in the VBA code, but they add it in places where it is not necessary to use them. This keyword will trigger some cell events like conditional formatting and animations which will hinder the performance of the macro. If you remove all the unnecessary selects, you can improve the performance of the macro. The following example will show you the code before and after you make a change to remove all the extra selects.

Before

Sheets("Order Details").Select

Columns("AC:AH").Select

Selection.ClearContents

After

Sheets("Order Details").Columns("AC:AH").ClearContents

Using The With Statement To Read Object Properties

When you work with objects, you should the With statement to decrease the number of times that the compiler reads the properties of the object. In the example below, see how the code changes when you use the With statement.

Before

Range("A1").Value = "Hello"

Range("A1").Font.Name = "Calibri"

Range("A1").Font.Bold = True

Range("A1").HorizontalAlignment = xlCenter

After

With Range("A1")

  .Value2 = "Hello"

  .HorizontalAlignment = xlCenter

      With .Font

        .Name = "Calibri"

.Bold = True

End With

End With

Using Arrays And Ranges

It is expensive to read and write to cells every time in Excel using VBA. You incur an overhead every time there is some movement of data between Excel and VBA. This means that you should always reduce the number of times the data moves between Excel and VBA. It is at such a time that ranges are useful. Instead of writing or reading the data individually to every cell within a loop, you can simply read the entire range into an array, and use that array in the loop. The example below will show you how you can use a range to read and write the values at once without having to read each cell individually.

Dim vArray As Variant

Dim iRow As Integer

Dim iCol As Integer

Dim dValue As Double

vArray = Range("A1:C10000").Value2 ' read all the values at once from the Excel cells, put into an array

For iRow = LBound(vArray, 1) To UBound(vArray, 1)

  For iCol = LBound(vArray, 2) To UBound(vArray, 2)

    dValue = vArray (iRow, iCol)

    If dValue > 0 Then

```
        dValue=dValue*dValue ' Change the values in the array, not
        the cells

        vArray(iRow, iCol) = dValue
```

End If

Next iCol

Next iRow

Range("A1:C10000").Value2 = vArray ' writes all the results back to the range at once

Use .Value2 Instead Of .Text or .Value

You can retrieve your values in different ways from a cell. The property you use to retrieve that information will have an impact on the performance of your code.

.Text

This is the most common property used to retrieve information from a cell. This will return a formatted value in the cell. It is complicated to only retrieve the formatted value of a cell and not just its value. It is for this reason that .Text is slow.

.Value

This keyword is an improvement over the .Text since this only retrieves the value and not the format of that value from the cell. If a cell is formatted as a currency or date, the .Value keyword will only return the VBA currency of VBA date which will truncate at decimal places.

.Value2

.Value2 on returns the underlying value of the cell. This function does not use any formatting and is faster than both the .Text and

.Value keywords. It works faster than the previous keywords when it comes to working with numbers, and is faster if you are using a variant array.

To learn more about these keywords, you should read the following blog post: https://fastexcel.wordpress.com/2011/11/30/text-vs-value-vs-value2-slow-text-and-how-to-avoid-it/

Avoid Using Copy And Paste

If you use a Macro Recorder to record the operations that also include copy and paste, the code will use these methods as a default operation. It is easier to avoid using the copy and paste method in VBA, and use some internal operations alone to perform those operations. It is easier to copy information faster if you only copy the values and not the formatting. You can also use these internal operations to copy the formulae. The following example will show you how you can avoid using the copy and paste options.

Before

Range("A1").Select

Selection.Copy

Range("A2").Select

ActiveSheet.Paste

After

' Approach 1: copy everything (formulas, values and formatting

Range("A1").Copy Destination:=Range("A2")

' Approach 2: copy values only

Range("A2").Value2 = Range("A1").Value2

' Approach 3: copy formulas only

Range("A2").Formula = Range("A1").Formula

If you think that the code is still functioning slowly, you can use the following fix: https://support.microsoft.com/en-in/help/2817672/macro-takes-longer-than-expected-to-execute-many-in

Use The Option Explicit Keyword To Catch Undeclared Variables

Option Explicit is one of the many Module directives that you can use in VBA. This directive will instruct VBA about how it should treat a code within a specific module. If you use Option Explicit, you should ensure that all the variables in the code are declared. If there is any variable that is not declared, it will throw a compile error. This will help you catch any variables that have been named incorrectly. It will also help to improve the performance of the macro where variables are defined at different times. You can set this by typing "Option Explicit" at the top of every module you write. Alternatively, you can check the "Require Variable Declaration" in the VBA editor under "Tools -> Options."

CHAPTER 11

How to Redirect the Flow

Using the GoTo Statement Correctly

The GoTo statement will allow you to redirect the flow of the program. Ensure that you understand how you can redirect the flow of the program, and see if there are different alternatives like using a loop. If you do not think there is any other way to do it, you can use the GoTo statement.

There are times when you will run into a situation where an existing program flow stops working, and you will need to disrupt it and move the compiler to another section of the code. This is where you can use the GoTo statement since it allows you to redirect the flow of the program. If you use this statement carefully, you can overcome different programming problems. That being said, the GoTo statement does lead to many other problems as well since it can be misused by the programmer. An amateur will want to use the GoTo statement since that will help them overlook programming errors. This means that they will begin to avoid fixing errors. Remember to use to GoTo statement with extreme care, and design the flow of your code well. You should also try to fix the errors in the code while writing it.

Loops

Never use the GoTo statement if you want to replace the end statement in a loop. The statements in the loop will always give the statements outside the loop an input value. Additionally, a standard loop statement always has the necessary keywords that will ensure that there are minimal or no errors.

Exits

You should always use the End statement instead of the GoTo statement if you want to exit a program.

Program Flow Problems

If there is any problem in the flow of the program that you have written, you must check the pseudo-code and then design the code again. This will help you ensure that the design for your code is correct. You may also need to change the design if necessary. Never make the assumption that the design is always correct, especially if you are doing this for the first time.

CHAPTER 12

Working with Excel Workbooks and Worksheets

The Workbook Collection

If you want to know the different workbooks you have open at a specific time, you can use the Workbooks Collection. You can also select the one workbook that you want to include in your program. This workbook is now a workbook object, and it provides all the general information about the file. You can use this object to access other objects in that document like Worksheet objects and Chart objects.

Example:

Public Sub WorkbookDemo()

' Holds the output data.

Dim Output As String

' Get the test workbook.

Dim ActiveWorkbook As Workbook

Set ActiveWorkbook =

```vb
Application.Workbooks("ExcelObjects.xls")
' Get the workbook name and location.
Output = "Name: " + ActiveWorkbook.Name + vbCrLf + _
"Full Name: " + ActiveWorkbook.FullName + vbCrLf + _
"Path: " + ActiveWorkbook.Path + vbCrLf + vbCrLf
' Holds the current sheet.
Dim CurrSheet As Worksheet
' Look for every sheet.
Output = "Worksheet List:" + vbCrLf
For Each CurrSheet In ActiveWorkbook.Worksheets
Output = Output + CurrSheet.Name + vbCrLf
Next
' Holds the current chart.
Dim CurrChart As Chart
' Look for every chart.
Output = Output + vbCrLf + "Chart List:" + vbCrLf
For Each CurrChart In ActiveWorkbook.Charts
Output = Output + CurrChart.Name + vbCrLf
Next
' Display the output.
MsgBox Output, vbInformation Or vbOKOnly, "Object List"
End Sub
```

The code begins by using the Application.Workbooks collection that will allow you to look at the different Workbook objects that you have open. You can also use it to retrieve one workbook object. Ensure that you use the correct name of the workbook that you want to open, and also include the extension of the file that you are trying to retrieve. The resulting workbook object will contain all that information about that document. This object will also provide some summary information about the document, and you can use that information to control and maintain the window. You can also add new elements or objects like worksheets to the workbook.

Once the workbook is accessed, the VBA compiler will use the ActiveWorkbook object to access the different worksheet objects that are present in the list. The code will always rely on the For Each... Next statement to access the different worksheet objects. You can also use an index if you want to access individual worksheets. The Active Worksheet will contain all the necessary methods and properties that you can use to manipulate the data in the worksheet, including embedded objects like pictures and charts. All the worksheets in the workbook will appear in the ActiveWorkbook object list by their object name. This will allow you to access them without using the Worksheet collection.

When you use the ActiveWorkbook object, you can only view the independent chart objects. You can also access any Chart object in the worksheet using the same technique that you use to access a worksheet object. The only difference here is that you cannot use the Worksheets collection, but will need to use the Charts collection. Ensure that the chart names will always appear in the object list when you look at the objects in the Active Workbook. This means that you do not need to use the Charts collection to access a chart.

The Worksheet Collection

One of the best ways to access any worksheet regardless of the situation is to use the Sheets collection. You should not follow the hierarchy of Excel objects if you want to identify the worksheet that you want to work with. If you access the worksheet that is at the top of the pyramid, it will mean that there are no objects that exist at the lower levels of the pyramid. Therefore, this technique can be looked at as a tradeoff.

You can always access any sheet type, and not only the worksheet that you will be using if you are using the Sheets collection. Any object, including a standalone Chart object, will also be a part of the worksheet. In the previous example, you will notice that the worksheet and chart objects are treated as separate objects.

Example:

Public Sub ListSheets()

' An individual entry.

Dim ThisEntry As Variant

' Holds the output data.

Dim Output As String

' Get the current number of worksheets.

Output = "Sheet Count: " + _

CStr(Application.Sheets.Count)

' List each worksheet in turn.

For Each ThisEntry In Application.Sheets

' Verify there is a sheet to work with.

```
If ThisEntry.Type = XlSheetType.xlWorksheet Then

Output = Output + vbCrLf + ThisEntry.Name

End If

Next

' Display the result.

MsgBox Output, _

vbInformation or vbOKOnly, _

"Worksheet List"

End Sub
```

In the above example, we are creating a Variant data type that will hold different types of sheets. If you use a Worksheet or Chart object, the code that you write will fail since you will not receive the type that you are looking for, although the type returned is valid. The issue with using the Variant data type is that the editor in VBA will not provide balloon help or automatic completion. You must ensure that the method you want to use is typed in correctly, and you always use the correct property names.

Once the necessary variables are all created, you will see the number of worksheets present in the workbook. Remember that this number not only includes the worksheets in the workbook, but also includes the charts in that workbook.

The For Each... Next Loop will retrieve every sheet in turn. You should also notice how the If... Then statement is being used to compare the values of the XlSheetType.xlWorksheet constant and the Variant data type. You can always separate a worksheet that you are using from the other objects in the Sheets collection type if necessary.

Charts Collection

You can use the Charts collection to design or build a custom chart if necessary. One of the advantages of creating a chart using a code is that it will not use too much space, and you can spend very little time when it comes to creating numerous charts.

Example:

Public Sub BuildChart()

' Create a new chart.

Dim NewChart As Chart

Set NewChart = Charts.Add(After:=Charts(Charts.Count))

' Change the name.

NewChart.Name = "Added Chart"

' Create a series for the chart.

Dim TheSeries As Series

NewChart.SeriesCollection.Add _

Source:=Worksheets("My Data Sheet").Range("A$3:B$8")

Set TheSeries = NewChart.SeriesCollection(1)

' Change the chart type.

TheSeries.ChartType = xl3DPie

' Change the series title.

TheSeries.Name = "Data from My Data Sheet"

' Perform some data formatting.

With TheSeries

.HasDataLabels = True

.DataLabels.ShowValue = True

.DataLabels.Font.Italic = True

.DataLabels.Font.Size = 14

End With

' Modify the chart's legend.

With NewChart

.HasLegend = True

.Legend.Font.Size = 14

End With

' Modify the 3-D view.

With NewChart

.Pie3DGroup.FirstSliceAngle = 90

.Elevation = 45

End With

' Format the chart title.

NewChart.ChartTitle.Font.Bold = True

NewChart.ChartTitle.Font.Size = 18

NewChart.ChartTitle.Format.Line.DashStyle _

= msoLineSolid

```
NewChart.ChartTitle.Format.Line.Style = msoLineSingle
NewChart.ChartTitle.Format.Line.Weight = 2
' Compute the optimal plot area size.
Dim Size As Integer
If NewChart.PlotArea.Height > NewChart.PlotArea.Width Then
Size = NewChart.PlotArea.Width
Else
Size = NewChart.PlotArea.Height
End If
' Reduce the plot area by 10%.
Size = Size - (Size * 0.1)
' Format the plot area.
With NewChart.PlotArea
.Interior.Color = RGB(255, 255, 255)
.Border.LineStyle = XlLineStyle.xlLineStyleNone
.Height = Size
.Width = Size
.Top = 75
.Left = 100
End With
```

```
' Format the labels.

Dim ChartLabels As DataLabel

Set ChartLabels = TheSeries.DataLabels(0)

ChartLabels.Position = xlLabelPositionOutsideEnd

End Sub
```

In the example above, you are instructing VBA to create a new chart. This chart will be the last chart in the workbook, but is not the last item in the workbook. This means that if a worksheet is created after the last chart, it will still appear in the object list. The NewChart.Name property will allow you to change the name that will appear at the bottom of the chart. This property will not change the name of the chart.

The chart is blank at this point, and you should add at least one of the series to the chart if you want to display any data on it. Remember that a pie chart can only display the data for one series at a time, but you can use different charts if you want to show multiple data series. For instance, you can show multiple data series using a bubble chart. In the next part of the data, you will create a data series using the information present in the worksheet "My Data Sheet." You will notice that the code will set the TheSeries variable equal to the output. Therefore, you must include an additional step that will help you obtain the new series from the Series Collection.

There are two columns that hold information in the Range property. If you are using Excel 2007 and above, the first column is used to define the XValues property in the chart. This property is used to determine the different entries in the legend for a pie chart. These values will appear at the bottom if you are using a Bar chart. In both the pie chart and the bar chart, you should display the labels on the screen. This will help you see their effect on the display area.

CHAPTER 13

Some Problems With Spreadsheets And How To Overcome Them

Most people use Excel to make a repository. This is because it is easy to make a list of small items for yourself or your colleagues in Excel. You may perhaps want to use some formulae to create something sophisticated. You may also want to use macros to automate the process of collecting and processing data. You can do this by typing an equal to sign in the cell before you write the formula. Excel will be your guide. There are some problems that everybody will face when it comes to using Excel, and that is its simplicity. You may start with a small project in Excel, and this project will grow until it becomes a daunting task. At this point, you may also face some issues with stability and speed, or some development problem that you cannot solve.

This chapter examines some of the common issues that people come across when they use spreadsheets, and also provides some solutions to tackle those problems. It will also tell you when you should switch to a database instead of sticking to Excel.

Multi-User Editing

When an Excel system begins to grow, you will quickly run into a problem where only one user can open the workbook at a time and make changes to it. Any other person who wants to open the workbook will be notified that someone already has the book open and that they can view the workbook as a read-only version or wait until the file is closed by the first user. Excel does promise to let you know when the first user has closed the file, but this is a hollow promise since Excel does not always check the status, and there are times when it may never give you an update. Even if it does give you an update, someone may already have opened the file before you.

You can get around this in the following ways:

- You should use Excel Online. This application is a web-based and abridged version of Microsoft Excel.

- Turn on the feature that will allow you to share the workbook.

- Split the workbook into smaller workbooks. This will allow different users to access different workbooks without causing any hindrances in the work.

Shared Workbooks

If you use Excel online, you can allow multiple users to edit the workbook at the same time. There is so much functionality that goes missing, which makes it a contender only for simple tasks. The shared workbook features in Excel will allow you to share the workbook between multiple users, but there are many restrictions. For instance, you cannot delete a group of cells or create a table in a shared workbook.

It is easy to walk around some restrictions, but for others, it is a matter of changing the structure of the entire workbook instead of using a workbook that has already been set up. These workarounds can, however, get in the way. As a result of this, it is impossible to use a workbook that is shared in the same way that you may use a single user workbook.

Any changes made in a shared workbook will be synchronized between the users every time the workbook is saved. These changes can be saved on a time schedule, meaning that a workbook can be saved or force saved every few minutes. The overhead of regular checking and savings every share user change is quite large. The size of the workbook can increase which will put a strain on your network, thereby slowing down every other system.

A shared workbook is prone to corruption. Microsoft office knows that this is the problem, but there is nothing much you can do about the issue. The alternative to this situation is to use Excel online since you can have multiple users working on the same workbook. Not many users will switch to excel online until Microsoft will remove all the restrictions on a shared workbook, and extend a multi-authoring tool to the Excel offline application.

Linked Workbooks

If you want to overcome the issue of multi-user editing, you should try to split the data across multiple workbooks. It is likely that these workbooks must be linked so that any value entered in one can be used in another. The links between workbooks also help to separate data using a logical method instead of using separate worksheets in one workbook.

Unfortunately, these links lead to instability and frustration. This is because the links need to be absolute or relative. In the case of absolute links, you will need to include the full path resource workbook while in the case of relative links, you only need to include the difference between the destination and source paths. This may sound sensible until you come across the rules the Excel decides to employ on when you can use each type of link, and when you can change them.

These rules are governed by numerous options. Some of these rules are dependent on whether the workbook was saved and whether it was saved before every link was inserted. There are times when Excel will automatically change the link when you open a workbook and use the save as option to copy the file. Excel may also change the links when you simply save the workbook down. One of the main disadvantages of using this option is that the links can break easily, and it is difficult to recover all the broken links. This is also a time-consuming affair since you cannot use the files that are affected by the broken links.

The linked data will only be updated when all the underlying files are open unless you edit links and update values. It is because of this that you may need to open 3 or 4 workbooks to ensure that all the information is flowing through in the right order. If you made a change in the value in the first workbook but open only the 3rd workbook, you will not see any changes because the second workbook still does not have the updated values.

It is logical to create a change in data, but this will increase the likelihood that the data is incorrect or/and when you open a workbook somebody else is already editing the underlying work. You can avoid the use of link workbooks, but there is a chance that you will end up entering the same data in more than one workbook. The danger with this is that you may type the data differently each time.

Data Validation

You must remember that any user can enter data on any computer system. People can transpose digits in numbers or mistype words with monotonous regularity. You must ensure that you check the data when it is entered or you will have a problem in the end.

Excel will always accept whatever any user types. Therefore, it is possible to set up a validation using lists, but it is impossible to maintain this list especially if that field is used in multiple places. For example, if a user should enter a customer reference number or a document ID they can enter the wrong record. To avoid this, it is always good to have some checks across the workbook. If there is no Data integrity, the system will be fatally compromised, which will affect the analysis.

You may already be suffering from this problem without having realized what the root cause is. Let us consider a situation where there is a list of invoices that you have entered in Excel Find the user has typed the name of every customer differently on every invoice. You got invoices to John limited, John Ltd and John. You are aware that these invoices point to the same company or customer, but Excel is not aware of this. This means that any analysis that you made using this data will always give you multiple results when they should only be one.

Navigation Issues

It is difficult to navigate through large workbooks. The number of sheet tabs in the bottom of the window is difficult to use and is a terrible way to find your way around the workbook. If there are many sheets in the workbook, and you cannot see all of them on the screen, it will be difficult for you to find what you are looking for. You can always click on the arrow to the left of your active sheet, but you will only see the first twenty sheets in that window. You cannot sort or group the list of sheets in any order.

Security Issues

You can add a lot of security features to an Excel workbook, but it is still going to have many problems. It is more important to work toward protecting the structure of the workbook, instead of worrying about the data. You can always lock some sheets and cells in the workbook to prevent some users from making any changes to the data or formulae. Regardless of whether you protect the sheet or not, if someone can see the data, they can make changes to it. You can avoid this by using some clever macro skills.

Speed Issues

You must remember that Excel is not the fastest application there is, and the programming language we use in Excel, VBA is slow and slightly sluggish when compared to the more professional languages like C and C#. This is because of the intended use of Excel and its flexibility. You should remember that Excel is a spreadsheet engine alone, and it can only be used to manage large volumes of data. This does not mean that you must always use Excel for this type of work. There are many other applications that you can use to perform such tasks since those applications were designed to perform these functions.

Enter the Database

If you are facing any of the issues that have been listed above, you should not ignore them. The answer or solution to these problems is to store the data in a structured manner. This means that we will need to start saving data in a database. This will allow you to think about your data in a logical manner. You have the ability to see how the data welding together and how you will need to interact with it to analyze the information.

You must, however, take heed. If you move from spreadsheets to databases, you should not duplicate the design of a spreadsheet. Instead, you should find a way to make the design better. There are some general database applications, listed below with which you can construct a simple solution. Alternatively, you can also use specialist database applications that allow you to switch from spreadsheet to databases within a few minutes point these applications are a better fit to big data.

For example, if you have a list of customers, their details, and any interaction you have had with these customers, then you should consider using a customer relationship management system. Customer relationship management system is a specialized database. Similarly, you can save accounts on packages like Sage and QuickBooks. There may be times when you cannot find an existing application to suit your needs. At such times you may need to build a database by yourself or request see IT department or any consultant to build the database for you.

The relational database is the most common type of database used in today's world. This database stores information or data in the form of tables which consists of columns and rows of data. Every row data will hold a separate item and every column will describe a different attribute of that item. For example, if the rows hold customer information, the columns can describe attributes like customer name and customer ID. All you need to do is enter the data once, and then you can use the same data to print on every invoice.

Every table in a relational database has a relationship between them. You can take the relationship between an invoice and the customer ID. Here you can always find an invoice that is related to a specific customer using the customer ID. Alternatively, you can also retrieve customer information from the invoice if necessary. All you need to do is enter the customer data of one in the database to create a record, and you can use that information across different invoices without having to type the data again. To use or create a database, you must define the tables and the relationships between those tables, and then define the type of layout you want to use to edit or list the data.

There are over a dozen applications that you can choose from. Some of the applications are easy to use and do the job for you. These applications will allow you to define the table, the data screen, and the reports. There are other applications that are more useful in specific areas but will require other tools to perform the job.

For example, some applications may be very powerful when comes defining a table and the relationship that table shares with the database and other tables, and it may also have some excellent analysis and reporting features. This application can, however, lack a tool which will allow you to define the data entry screen. An obvious example of such an application is Microsoft SQL. As is the case with large database systems, the SQL server will only take care of the back-end annual expect you to use, and other tools like visual studio to develop or maintain the front-end.

Choosing The Right Database

Access

Microsoft Access is one of the oldest databases available. This is easy to use and is extremely easy to abuse. You can design screens, reports, and tables from scratch or use an existing template. Some of the templates in Access do not teach you some good practices, but they will help you get started quickly. The programming and screen features and options are sophisticated, and you can deploy the application on the intranet without having to rely on sharing the files with users.

SharePoint

SharePoint is a document storage application and a database. This application can be used to compile and link simple lists. You can use the form designer to customize your dashboard, but it is important to remember that it is not a sophisticated application to use. SharePoint has the ability to suck the information from Excel and put it into a custom list. This makes it a useful application since everybody in your network will have access to the list. You can choose to add some security features which will restrict the access for some people. SharePoint can also send you an alert email when someone makes a change – adds, deletes or edits – to a record. You can also synchronize the information with Outlook if you have some data that concerns a person, calendar or task.

Zoho Creator

There is a database application that you can use in the Zoho office services available on the Internet. You can drag and drop the required layout in an easy way. This will also help you decide how the work should flow and what the interaction can be like. Since this is a web application, the data you use and the applications you develop can be found anywhere. Therefore, you should use the simple security features that this application provides to keep your data private. Zoho charges you per month but will allow you to store only some records depending on the price you choose to pay. If you want to use advanced features like email integration, you will need to pay an additional amount of money.

CHAPTER 14

How To Use Data From Excel

There are times when you will need to manually copy the data from one Excel file to the next. You can always automate this process if necessary, and also ensure that the data is copied correctly. You can also verify if the copied data has no duplications and no figure is entered into an incorrect location. This will help you save a lot of time.

You can either write the code in the Workbook_Open() event or include a function in the ThisWorkBook object to perform this function. When you write the code in the former event, the compiler will ensure that all the figures are copied over correctly when the source file is open.

When you want to develop the code, you should open the destination Excel file, and press the shortcut Alt+F8. The ThisWorkBook module can be found under the Microsoft Excel Objects in the

Project Explorer window. You should now open the window and choose the "Workbook" object from the object dropdown[46].

Option Explicit

Private Sub Workbook_Open()

  Call ReadDataFromCloseFile

End Sub

Sub ReadDataFromCloseFile()

    On Error GoTo ErrHandler

    Application.ScreenUpdating = False

    Dim src As Workbook

    ' OPEN THE SOURCE EXCEL WORKBOOK IN "READ ONLY MODE".

    Set src = Workbooks.Open("C:\Q-SALES.xlsx", True, True)

    ' GET THE TOTAL ROWS FROM THE SOURCE WORKBOOK.

    Dim iTotalRows As Integer

    iTotalRows = src.Worksheets("sheet1").Range("B1:B" & Cells(Rows.Count, "B").End(xlUp).Row).Rows.Count

    ' COPY DATA FROM SOURCE (CLOSE WORKGROUP) TO THE DESTINATION WORKBOOK.

---

[46] How to Get Values From Another Sheet in Excel Using VBA. (2019). Retrieved from https://chartio.com/resources/tutorials/how-to-get-values-from-another-sheet-in-excel-using-vba/

```
    Dim iCnt As Integer    ' COUNTER.

    For iCnt = 1 To iTotalRows

Worksheets("Sheet1").Range("B" & iCnt).Formula = 

    src.Worksheets("Sheet1").Range("B" & iCnt).Formula

    Next iCnt

    ' CLOSE THE SOURCE FILE.

    src.Close False         ' FALSE - DON'T SAVE THE SOURCE FILE.

    Set src = Nothing

ErrHandler:

    Application.EnableEvents = True

    Application.ScreenUpdating = True

End Sub
```

Property Application.ScreenUpdating

In the first line of the code, you will see that the Application.ScreenUpdating property is set to false. This will help you improve the speed of the macro that was written.

Open the Source File and Read Data

The next step is to open the source workbook that you are copying the information from. Remember that Excel will open the source file in the read only state, which will ensure that no changes are made to the source file.

Set src = Workbooks.Open("C:\Q-SALES.xlsx", True, True)

Once you have obtained the necessary information, the compiler will count the number of rows that are present in the source Excel workbook. This loop will run, and the data will be copied accurately from the source to the destination.

' COPY DATA FROM SOURCE (CLOSE WORKGROUP) TO THE DESTINATION FILE.

For iCnt = 1 To iTotalRows

   Worksheets("Sheet1").Range("B" & iCnt).Formula =

     src.Worksheets("Sheet1").Range("B" & iCnt).Formula

Next iCnt

Once the data has been copied over, you can set the property Application.ScreenUpdating to true.

CHAPTER 15

How to Manipulate Data In Excel

Every macro will process the code that is written in to manipulate and manage large volumes of data. The last chapter showed you how you can use VBA to format specific cells and fields in Excel to meet your criteria.

The following is an example of a VBA script:

Sub ConfigureLogic()

Dim qstEntries

Dim dqstEntries

Dim qstCnt, dqstCnt

qstEntries = Range("QualifiedEntry").Count

qst = qstEntries - WorksheetFunction.CountIf(Range("QualifiedEntry"), "")

ReDim QualifiedEntryText(qst)

'MsgBox (qst)

dqstEntries = Range("DisQualifiedEntry").Count

dqst = dqstEntries - WorksheetFunction.CountIf(Range("DisQualifiedEntry"), "")

```
ReDim DisqualifiedEntryText(dqst)

'MsgBox (dqst)

For qstCnt = 1 To qst

QualifiedEntryText(qstCnt) = ThisWorkbook.Worksheets("Qualifiers").Range("J" & 8 + qstCnt).value

'MsgBox (QualifiedEntryText(qstCnt))

logging ("Configured Qualified Entry entry #" & qstCnt & " as {" & QualifiedEntryText(qstCnt) & "}")

Next

For dqstCnt = 1 To dqst

DisqualifiedEntryText(dqstCnt) = ThisWorkbook.Worksheets("Qualifiers").Range("M" & 8 + dqstCnt).value

'MsgBox (DisqualifiedEntryText(dqstCnt))

logging ("Configured DisQualified Entry entry #" & qstCnt & " as {" & DisqualifiedEntryText(dqstCnt) & "}")

Next

includeEntry = ThisWorkbook.Worksheets("Qualifiers").Range("IncludeSibling").value

'MsgBox (includeEntry)

logging ("Entrys included in search - " & includeEntry)

End Sub
```

How to Analyze and Manipulate Data In A Spreadsheet

If you want to analyze data using VBA, you should look at the different macro settings in Excel. You must ensure that all the settings are as per the requirement. You must also ensure that every macro setting is activated in Excel. Now, you should create a worksheet and call it 'Qualifiers.' This is the worksheet that we will be using to ensure that the data is accurate and meets all the requirements. You can then set up the necessary qualifiers using the code that you have written. Remember that you cannot copy and paste these qualifiers, but will need to enter them into the system manually.

ThisWorkbook.Worksheets("Qualifiers").Range("J" & 8 + qstCnt).value

How To Construct An Array And Locate The Range

In the above function, the range will start from Cell J9. The function notes 8, but the range is 9 since we have declared the qstCnt to be 1 using the following code:

For qstCnt = 1 To qst

It is because of this statement that the list will start at 9.

If you want to construct an array using the entries in the Qualifiers worksheet, you should add random words or numbers between cells J9 and J13, including those cells. When the rows are complete, you can find and manipulate the data in Excel.

Private Sub CountSheets()

Dim sheetcount

Dim WS As Worksheet

sheetcount = 0

logging ("*****Starting Scrub*********")

For Each WS In ThisWorkbook.Worksheets

sheetcount = sheetcount + 1

If WS.Name = "Selected" Then

'need to log the date and time into sheet named "Logging"

ActionCnt = ActionCnt + 1

logging ("Calling sheet: " & WS.Name)

scrubsheet (sheetcount)

Else

ActionCnt = ActionCnt + 1

logging ("Skipped over sheet: " & WS.Name)

End If

Next WS

'MsgBox ("ending")

ActionCnt = ActionCnt + 1

logging ("****Scrub DONE!")

Application.ScreenUpdating = True

End Sub

The following example will show you how you can write a macro for a working tab counter.

Dim sheetcount

Dim WS As Worksheet

```
sheetcount = 0

logging ("*****Starting Scrub*********")

For Each WS In ThisWorkbook.Worksheets

sheetcount = sheetcount + 1
```

When you initialize the sheet count variable, you should first set it to zero before you restart the counter. You can also use the logging() subroutine to keep track of all the actions in the qualifiers tab to make the correct selections. The For loop in the above example will set up the counting variable in the Active Workbook. Once you initialize WS, it will make the worksheet that you are currently in the active worksheet. Since this module is unnamed, it will run in any workbook. If you have many workbooks open, this module may run in an incorrect workbook. If you want to avoid any errors, you should name the workbook that you want the module to run in.

When the loop runs, it will add another variable to the sheet count and keep a track of the tabs. We will then move to

```
If WS.Name = "Selected" Then

'need to log the date and time into sheet named "Logging"

ActionCnt = ActionCnt + 1

logging ("Calling sheet: " & WS.Name)

scrubsheet (sheetcount)

Else

ActionCnt = ActionCnt + 1

logging ("Skipped over sheet: " & WS.Name)

End If
```

In this section of the code, we are trying to look for the Selected tab. VBA will run the subroutine if the variable WS is the same as the Selected Worksheet. If the variable is not the same, the sheet will not be looked at by the compiler and the action will be looked at and counted. The code above is an example of how you can write macro to locate a specific tab or count the number of tabs in the macro.

In the next parts of this chapter, we will look at the different ways in which you can manipulate the data in Excel.

Different Ways To Manipulate Data

Count The Number Of Sheets In A Workbook[47]

Dim TAB

For Each TAB In ThisWorkbook.Worksheets

'some routine here

Next

Filter By Using Advanced Criteria

Range("A2:Z99").Sort key1:=Range("A5"), order1:=xlAscending, Header:=xlNo

Find The Last Column, Cell Or Row On A Worksheet

Dim cellcount

cellcount = Cells(ThisWorkbook.Worksheets("worksheet").Rows.Count, 1).End(xlUp).Row

---

[47] How To Manipulate Data in Excel Using VBA. (2019). Retrieved from https://ccm.net/faq/53497-how-to-manipulate-data-in-excel-using-vba

Getting Values From Another Worksheet

dim newvalue

newvalue = ThisWorkbook.Worksheets("worksheet").Range("F1").value

Apply Auto-Fit To A Column

Columns("A:A").EntireColumn.AutoFit

Adding Named Ranges to Specific Sheets

ThisWorkbook.Worksheets("worksheet").Names.Add Name:="Status", RefersToR1C1:="=worksheet!C2"

Insert Rows Into A Worksheet

Dim Row, Column

Cells(Row, Column).EntireRow.Select

Selection.Insert

Copy An Entire Row For Pasting

ActiveSheet.Range("A1").EntireRow.Select

Selection.Copy

Delete An Entire Row

ActiveSheet.Range("A1").EntireRow.Select

Selection.Delete

Inserting A Column Into A Worksheet

Dim Row, Column

Cells(Row, Column).EntireColumn.Select

Selection.Insert

Insert Multiple Columns Into A Worksheet

Dim insertCnt

Dim Row, Column

For insertCnt = 1 To N

ThisWorkbook.Worksheets("worksheet").Select

Cells(Row, Column).EntireColumn.Select

Selection.Insert

Next

Select A Specific Sheet

ThisWorkbook.Worksheets("worksheet").Select

Compare Values In A Range

Dim firstrange

Dim Logictest

Logictest = "some word or value"

If (Range(firstrange).value = Logictest) then

'some routine here

End If

CHAPTER 16

Resources For VBA Help

You cannot expect to become a VBA expert in a day. It is a journey and you will need to practice a lot before you become an expert. The best part about coding in Excel VBA is that there are many resources that you can use to improve your knowledge in Excel. This chapter covers some of the best places you can visit and some of the best resources you can use if you need a push in the right direction.

Allow Excel To Write The Code For You

If you have read the previous chapters, you know that you can use the macro recorder to help you with understanding your code. When you record any macro or the steps you want to automate using a record macro, Excel will write the underlying code for you. Once you record the code, you can review it and see what the recorder has done. You can then convert the code that the recorder has written into something that will suit your needs.

For instance, if you need to write a macro to refresh a pivot table or all pivot tables in your workbook and clear all the filters in the pivot table, it will get difficult to write the code from scratch. You can instead start recording the macro, and refresh every pivot table and remove all the filters yourself. When you stop recording the macro, you can review it and make the necessary changes to the code.

For a new Excel user, it would seem that the Help system is an add-in that always returns a list of topics that do not have anything to do with the topic you are looking for. The truth is that when you learn how to use the Help System correctly, it is the easiest and the fastest way to obtain more information about a topic. There are two basic tenets that you must keep in mind:

The Location Matters When You Ask For Help

There are two Help Systems in Excel: one that provides help on the different features in Excel and the other that provides information on some VBA programming topics. Excel will not perform a global search but will throw the criteria against the Help system which is in your current location. This means that you will receive the help that you need depending on which area of Excel you are working in. If you want help on VBA and macros, you need to be in the Visual Basic Environment (VBE) when you look for information. This will ensure that the keyword search is performed on the correct help system.

Choose Online Help Over Offline Help

When you look for some information on a topic, Excel will see if you are connected to the Internet. If your system is connected to the Internet, Excel will return results using some online content on Microsoft's website. Otherwise, Excel will use the help files that are stored offline in Microsoft office. It is always good to choose online help since the content is more detailed. It also includes updated information and the links to other resources that you can use.

Using Code From The Internet

The secret to building large programs is that you never have to write new code again. The macro syntax or the entire program that you want to use is certainly available on the Internet. This means that you never have to build anything from scratch. You can always use the code that is available on the Internet and apply that code to build different applications.

If you are stuck with creating or writing a macro for a specific task, all you need to do is describe the task you want to accomplish using Google Search. All you need to do is add the words "Excel VBA" before you describe your requirement.

For instance, if you want to write a macro that will allow you to delete all the blank rows in a worksheet, you should look for "How to delete blank rows in Excel using VBA?". You can bet a whole years' worth of salary that someone somewhere has already developed code for the same problem. There is probably an example that is available on the Internet which will give you an idea of what you need to do. This way you can simply build your own macro.

Leveraging Excel VBA User Forums

When you find yourself in trouble, you should post a question on a forum and then get guidance based on your requirement. A user forum is an online community that revolves around specific topics. You can ask numerous questions in these forums and get advice from experts on how you should solve some problems. The people answering your questions are volunteers who are passionate about helping the community solve some real-world problems.

There are many forums that are dedicated to helping people with Excel. If you want to find such a forum, you should type "Excel Forum" in Google Search. Let us look at some tips you can use to get the most out of the user form.

You should always read the forum and follow all the rules before you begin. These rules will often include some advice on how you should post your questions and also the etiquette you should follow.

Always check if the question you want to ask has already been answered. You should try to save some time by looking at the archives. Now, take a moment to look at the forum and verify if any of the questions you want answers to have already been asked.

You should use accurate and concise titles for any of your questions. You should never create a forum question using an abstract title like "Please Help" or "Need advice."

You should always ensure that the scope of your question is narrow. You should never ask questions like "How should I build an accounting macro in Excel."

You should always be patient, and remember that the people who are answering your questions are those who have a day job. You should always give the community sufficient time to answer the questions.

You should always check often when you post your questions. You will probably receive some information for more details about your question. You should always return to your post to either respond to some follow-up questions or review the answer.

You should always thank the person who has answered your question. If you were to receive an answer which helps you, you should thank the expert who has helped you.

Leveraging on Excel VBA Blogs And Articles

There are some dedicated Excel Gurus who have shared their knowledge through their blogs. These blogs are treasure troves of tricks and tips. They have some information that you can use to build your skills. The best part of using these blogs is that they are free to use.

These blogs do not necessarily answer your specific questions, but they offer many articles that you can use to advance your knowledge of VBA and Excel. These blogs can also provide some general guidance on how you can apply Excel in different situations. Let us look at a few popular Excel blogs:

ExcelGuru

ExcelGuru is a blog that was set up by Ken Puls. He is an Excel MVP who shares all his knowledge on his blog. Apart from the blog, Ken also offers many learning resources you can use to improve your knowledge in Excel.

Org

Org is a blog that was set up by Purna Chandoo Duggirala. He is an Excel expert from India who joined the scene in 2007. His blog offers innovative solutions and some free templates that will make you "awesome in Excel."

Contextures

Debra Dalgleish is the owner of a popular Excel website and is great with Microsoft Excel. She has included close to 350 topics on her website, and there will definitely be something that you can read.

DailyDose

The DailyDose is a blog that is owned by Dick Kusleika. It is the longest running Excel blog, and Dick is an expert at Excel VBA. He has written articles and blogs for over ten years.

MrExcel

Bill Jelen always uses Excel to solve any problems he has at work. He offers a large library of training resources and over thousands of free videos.

Mining YouTube For Some Excel VBA Training Videos

If you know that there are some training videos that are available on the Internet, and these sessions are better than articles, you should look for those videos. There are many channels that are run by amazing experts that are passionate for sharing knowledge. You will be pleasantly surprised to see the quality of those videos.

Attending A Live Online Excel VBA Training Class

Live training sessions are a great way to absorb good Excel knowledge form a diverse set of people. The instructor is providing some information on different techniques, but the discussions held after the class will leave you with a wealth of ideas and tips. You may have never thought of these ideas ever before. If you can survive these classes, you should always consider attending more of these sessions. Here are some websites that you can use for such sessions:

- Org
- ExcelHero
- ExcelJet
- Learning From The Microsoft Office Developer Center For Help With VBA

You should use the Microsoft Office Dev Center to get some help on how to start programming in Office products. The website is slightly difficult to navigate, but it is worth it to look at the sample code, free resources, step-by-step instructions, tools, and much more.

Dissecting Other Excel Files In Your Organization

Previous employees or current employees may have created files that already answer some of your questions. You should try to open different Excel files that contain the right macros, and also look at how these macros function. Then see how other employees in the organization develop macros for different applications. You should try not to go through the macro line-by-line but should look for some new techniques that may have been used.

You can also try to identify new tricks that you may have never thought of. You will probably also stumble upon some large chunks of code that you can implement or copy into your workbooks.

Ask The Local Excel Guru

Is there an excel genius in your department, company, community, or organization? If yes, you should become friends with that person now. That person will become your own personal guru. Excel experts love to share their knowledge, so you should never be afraid to approach an expert if you have any questions or want to seek advice on how you can solve some problems.

CHAPTER 17

Mistakes To Avoid

If you are reading this chapter, you will be familiar with Excel VBA. It is easy for anybody to make mistakes when they write a code in VBA. These mistakes will cost you greatly. This chapter lists the common mistakes that most VBA amateurs make.

Not Using Arrays

An interesting mistake that most VBA programmers make is that they try to process all the functions in a large nested loop. They filter the data down through the different rows and columns in the worksheet during the process of calculation. This method can work, but it can lead to performance troubles. If you have to perform the same function repeatedly, the efficiency of the macro will decrease. When you loop through the same column and you extract the values every single time, you are not only affecting the macro, but also affecting the processor. An efficient way to handle a list of numbers is to use an array.

If you have not used an array before, let me introduce it to you now. An array is a set of elements that have the same data type. Each element in the array is given an index. You must use this index to refer to the element in the array. An array can be defined by using the following statement: Dim MyArray (12) as Integer. This will create an array with 12 indices and variables that you will need to fill. Let us look at how a loop with an array will look[48] like:

Sub Test1()

    Dim x As Integer

    intNumRows = Range("A2", Range("A2").End(xldown)).Rows.Count

    Range("A2").Select

    For x = 1 To intNumRows

    arrMyArray(x-1) = Range("A" & str(x)).value

    ActiveCell.Offset(1, 0).Select

    Next

End Sub

In this example, the code is processing through every cell in the range before it performs the calculation function.

Using .Select or .Activate

You do not have to always use the .Select or .Activate functions when you write code in VBA. You may want to use these functions since the Macro Recorder generates them. These functions are unnecessary for the following reasons:

---

[48] 7 Common VBA Mistakes to Avoid - Spreadsheets Made Easy. (2019). Retrieved from https://www.spreadsheetsmadeeasy.com/7-common-vba-mistakes-to-avoid/

- These functions may lead to the repainting of the screen. If you use the following function Sheets("Sheet1").Activate, Excel will redraw the screen so you can see Sheet1. This will lead to a slow macro.

- These functions will confuse users since you will be manipulating the workbook when the user is working on it. There are some users who will worry that they are being hacked.

You should use these functions only when you want to bring the user to a specific cell or worksheet. Otherwise, you should delete the line of code since it will be doing more harm than good.

Using Variant Type

Another mistake that most programmers make is to use one Type when they are actually using another. If you look at the following code, you will think that a, b, and c are of the Long type. Well, that is incorrect since the variables a and b are of the Variant type. This means that they can be any data type, and can change from one type to another.

It is dangerous to have a variant type since it will become difficult for you to identify the bugs in your code. You should always avoid Variant types in VBA. There are some functions that will need the use of a Variant type, but you should avoid them if you can.

Not Using Application.ScreenUpdating = False

When you make a change to a cell or a group of cells in your code, Excel will need to repaint the screen to show the user the changes.

This will make your macros slow. When you write a macro the next time, you should use the following lines of code[49]:

Public Sub MakeCodeFaster()

    Application.ScreenUpdating = False

    ' Block of code

    ' This setting should always be reset back

    Application.ScreenUpdating = True

End Sub

Referencing the Worksheet Name With a String

[50] People will refer to a worksheet using a String. Look at the following example:

Public Sub SheetReferenceExample()

    Dim ws As Worksheet

    Set ws = Sheets("Sheet1")

    Debug.Print ws.Name

End Sub

---

[49] 7 Common VBA Mistakes to Avoid - Spreadsheets Made Easy. (2019). Retrieved from https://www.spreadsheetsmadeeasy.com/7-common-vba-mistakes-to-avoid/

[50] 7 Common VBA Mistakes to Avoid - Spreadsheets Made Easy. (2019). Retrieved from https://www.spreadsheetsmadeeasy.com/7-common-vba-mistakes-to-avoid/

This does seem harmless does it not. In most cases, it is harmless. Imagine that you give another person this workbook, and that person decides to rename the sheet to "Report." When he tries to run the macro, the macro will look for "Sheet1," which no longer exists. Therefore, this macro will not work. You should choose to reference the sheet by using an object instead of using the "Sheets" collection. To be more resilient, let us use the following block of code:

```
Public Sub SheetReferenceExample()

    Dim ws As Worksheet

    Set ws = Sheet1 ' used to be Sheets("Sheet1")

    Debug.Print ws.Name

End Sub
```

If you want to rename Sheet1 to something more meaningful, you can go to the VBA Project properties window and make a change to the name of the module. Once you rename the module, you will also need to update the VBA code.

Not Qualifying the Range References

[51]This is a common mistake that most people make when they write their code, and it is a real pain to debug this error. This error comes up when you do not qualify the range reference in the VBA code. You may wonder what I mean when I say range reference.

When you say Range("A1"), which sheet do you think the code is referring to? It is referring to the Activesheet. This means that the

---

[51] 7 Common VBA Mistakes to Avoid - Spreadsheets Made Easy. (2019). Retrieved from https://www.spreadsheetsmadeeasy.com/7-common-vba-mistakes-to-avoid/

compiler will look at cell A1 in the worksheet that the user is referring to. This is harmless on most occasions, but there are times when you may add more features to your code. These features make it hard for the compiler to execute the code. When the user or even you run the code, and you click on another worksheet, the code will behave differently. Let us look at the following example:

Public Sub FullyQualifyReferences()

    Dim fillRange As Range

    Set fillRange = Range("A1:B5")

    Dim cell As Range

    For Each cell In fillRange

    Range(cell.Address) = cell.Address

    Application.Wait (Now + TimeValue("0:00:01"))

    DoEvents

    Next cell

End Sub

Run the code in VBA and see what happens. If you do not specify the worksheet when you use the Range() function, Excel will assume that you are looking at the active sheet. To avoid this, you should make a slight change to your code. All you need to do is change Range(cell.Address) = cell.Address to Data.Range(cell.Address) = cell.Address.

In the second statement, data refers to the sheet object. There are other ways to do this, but I wanted to use a simple example which did not need the addition of too much code.

Writing a Big Function

If you go back to some of the old functions you may have written, you will notice that they are very long. You will need to continue to scroll until you reach the end of the function.

You should remember that the function you write should fit your screen. You should be able to view the code without having to scroll. You must ensure that you keep the methods short by creating sub procedures or helper functions.

Using Nested For or If Statements

[52]You may have read earlier that you can include many levels of nesting when you write your code. Do you think that is a good idea? You will need to add comments and indent the code to ensure that another user can read your code. If you are unsure of what I mean by nesting, let us look at the following example:

Public Sub WayTooMuchNesting()

    Dim updateRange As Range

    Set updateRange = Sheet2.Range("B2:B50")

    Dim cell As Range

    For Each cell In updateRange

    If (cell.Value > 1) Then

    If (cell.Value < 100) Then

---

[52] 7 Common VBA Mistakes to Avoid - Spreadsheets Made Easy. (2019). Retrieved from https://www.spreadsheetsmadeeasy.com/7-common-vba-mistakes-to-avoid/

```
        If (cell.Offset(0, 1).Value = "2x Cost") Then

            cell.Value = cell.Value * 2

        Else

            ' do nothing

        End If

      End If

    End If

    Next cell

End Sub
```

This is certainly not a clean code. If you use more than three levels of nesting, you have gone too far. To reduce the number of nesting levels, you should invert the condition in your If statement. In the example above, the code will make a change if a bunch of statements pass. You can invert this to ensure that the compiler will only execute the statements for the opposite case. That way you can skip the many levels of nesting.

Let us look at the updated[53] version of the above example.

```
Public Sub ReducedNesting()

    Dim updateRange As Range

  Set updateRange = Sheet2.Range("B2:B50")
```

---

[53] 7 Common VBA Mistakes to Avoid - Spreadsheets Made Easy. (2019). Retrieved from https://www.spreadsheetsmadeeasy.com/7-common-vba-mistakes-to-avoid/

```
Dim cell As Range

For Each cell In updateRange

    If (cell.Value <= 1) Then GoTo NextCell

    If (cell.Value >= 100) Then GoTo NextCell

    If (cell.Offset(0, 1).Value <> "2x Cost") Then GoTo NextCell

    cell.Value = cell.Value * 2

NextCell:

Next cell

End Sub
```

You can also combine the If statements in the code above if you wish.

Conclusion

On that note, we have come to the end of this book. I want to thank you once again for purchasing the book and I sincerely hope you find it informative.

This book will help you gain a good understanding of what VBA is and how you can use it to automate processes in Excel. The book also helps you understand how you can fix code or handle errors.

I hope this book helps you automate the many processes that you do in Excel.

Good Luck!

References

(2019). Retrieved from http://users.iems.northwestern.edu/~nelsonb/IEMS435/VBA Primer.pdf

10 Resources for Excel VBA Help - dummies. (2019). Retrieved from https://www.dummies.com/software/microsoft-office/excel/10-resources-for-excel-vba-help/

7 Common VBA Mistakes to Avoid - Spreadsheets Made Easy. (2019). Retrieved from https://www.spreadsheetsmadeeasy.com/7-common-vba-mistakes-to-avoid/

9 quick tips to improve your VBA macro performance. (2019). Retrieved from https://techcommunity.microsoft.com/t5/Excel/9-quick-tips-to-improve-your-VBA-macro-performance/td-p/173687

Banik, A. (2019). Excel VBA – Read Data from a Closed Excel File or Workbook without Opening it. Retrieved from https://www.encodedna.com/excel/copy-data-from-closed-excel-workbook-without-opening.htm

Conditional Logic in VBA. (2019). Retrieved from http://codevba.com/learn/condition_statements.htm#.W-UNZ5MzbIU

Conditional Statements in Excel VBA - If, Case, For, Do Loops. (2019). Retrieved from https://analysistabs.com/excel-vba/conditional-statements/

Conditional Statements in Excel VBA - If, Case, For, Do Loops. (2019). Retrieved from https://analysistabs.com/excel-vba/conditional-statements/

Error Handling In VBA. (2019). Retrieved from http://www.cpearson.com/excel/errorhandling.htm

Excel Macro Troubleshooting Tips. (2019). Retrieved from https://www.contextures.com/excelvbatips.html

Excel VBA - Introduction. (2019). Retrieved from https://www.tutorialspoint.com/excel_vba_online_training/excel_vba_introduction.asp

Excel VBA Loops, with examples. For Loop; Do While Loop; Do Until Loop. (2019). Retrieved from http://www.globaliconnect.com/excel/index.php?option=com_content&view=article&id=122:excel-vba-loops-with-examples-for-loop-do-while-loop-do-until-loop&catid=79&Itemid=475

Excel VBA Primer. (2019). Retrieved from http://ce270.groups.et.byu.net/syllabus/vbaprimer/intro/index.php

Excel VBA Tutorial Introduction: How to get started. (2019). Retrieved from http://www.easyexcelvba.com/introduction.html

Getting Started With VBA — The Spreadsheet Guru. (2019). Retrieved from https://www.thespreadsheetguru.com/getting-started-with-vba/

Gomez, J. (2019). Excel VBA Sub Procedures: The Complete Tutorial. Retrieved from https://powerspreadsheets.com/vba-sub-procedures/

Gomez, J. (2019). VBA Loops Explained: Complete Tutorial On 6 Essential Excel VBA Loops. Retrieved from https://powerspreadsheets.com/excel-vba-loops/#What-Is-An-Excel-VBA-Loop

Kelly, P. (2019). How to Easily Extract From Any String Without Using VBA InStr - Excel Macro Mastery. Retrieved from https://excelmacromastery.com/vba-instr/#Example_3_Checkif_a_filename_is_valid

Kelly, P. (2019). The Ultimate Guide to VBA String Functions - Excel Macro Mastery. Retrieved from https://excelmacromastery.com/vba-string-functions/#How_To_Use_Compare

Kelly, P. (2019). The Ultimate Guide to VBA String Functions - Excel Macro Mastery. Retrieved from https://excelmacromastery.com/vba-string-functions/#Scarching_Within_a_String

Loop in Excel VBA. (2019). Retrieved from https://www.excel-easy.com/vba/loop.html

Mathier, S. (2019). VBA Course: Introduction. Retrieved from https://www.excel-pratique.com/en/vba/introduction.php

MS Excel: How to use the IF-THEN-ELSE Statement (VBA). (2019). Retrieved from https://www.techonthenet.com/excel/formulas/if_then.php

Read or Get Data from Worksheet Cell to VBA in Excel - ANALYSISTABS - Innovating Awesome Tools for Data Analysis!. (2019). Retrieved from https://analysistabs.com/excel-vba/read-get-data-from-cell-worksheet/

String Manipulation in Excel VBA. (2019). Retrieved from https://www.excel-easy.com/vba/string-manipulation.html

Strings in VBA. (2019). Retrieved from http://codevba.com/learn/strings.htm#.W-RAHNUzaCg

Ten VBA Tips and Tricks. (2019). Retrieved from http://what-when-how.com/excel-vba/ten-vba-tips-and-tricks/

Variables in Excel VBA. (2019). Retrieved from https://www.excel-easy.com/vba/variables.html

VBA Conditional Statements. (2019). Retrieved from https://www.excelfunctions.net/vba-conditional-statements.html

VBA Loops - For, Do-While and Do-Until Loops. (2019). Retrieved from https://www.excelfunctions.net/vba-loops.html

VBA Primer (Excel). (2019). Retrieved from http://mcise.uri.edu/jones/ise325/vba%20primer.htm

VBA Strings. (2019). Retrieved from https://www.tutorialspoint.com/vba/vba_strings.htm

VBA Sub Procedure. (2019). Retrieved from https://www.tutorialspoint.com/vba/vba_sub_procedure.htm

Wells, R. (2019). Declaring Variables in VBA - wellsr.com. Retrieved from https://wellsr.com/vba/excel/vba-declare-variable/

Made in the USA
Coppell, TX
13 December 2019